Word in the Heart

Teacher's Manual

Junior

Year 4: Quarters 1-4

Table of Contents

4:1 The Sermon on the Mount

4:2 Leaders in Israel

4:3 The Beginning of Things

4:3 The Apostles

ISBN 10: 1-58427288-0
ISBN 13: 978-158427288-5

Notes

An Educator Talks About Your Junior Student

A teacher must understand his students in order to succeed in their instruction and to accomplish what is needed with them and the Kingdom of God. Study each student individually and try to understand his personal and individual needs and then consider the group as a whole so that you may instruct them more effectively.

Physical Characteristics

Physically your students are strong, healthy, and alert. They are active and exuberant and, with the normal energy of those in grades four, five, and six, may amaze you with their vitality. At this age they are beginning to experiment in independence and to attempt greater degrees of personal freedom and individual rights. They may be inclined to be less tidy than you would prefer—expecially the boys—and more interested in being outside and active than sitting in a classroom.

Mental Characteristics

Mentally they are exceedingly alert, and the brightest may challenge even the best of teachers with thought-provoking questions and comments. Your students will be able to find Bible references, answer workbook questions, and read and explain Bible verses in class. Memorizing is done easily at this age and should be encouraged at every class period. They are eager for information but will be critical and questioning. You should be ready to prove every point with Scripture. Your students can be creative if you give them your time, interest, and understanding. They will be interested in projects that will enhance the Bible knowledge. Their interest spans and powers of concentration have improved considerably over the primary level student.

Social Characteristics

Socially your students are becoming discriminating. They will tend to separate into small groups—especially girls with girls and boys with boys. The boys will strongly prefer the male companions and pretend great dislike for girls. They will be embarrassed if strongly urged to work with girls. They can be encouraged to high standards and will expect complete fairness in all treatment. At this age they must be taught at every opportunity to respect all authorities that are over them. Bible stories that emphasize action, courage, and obedience to God will make the deepest impressions on them.

Spiritual Characteristics

Spiritually your students are at an age to understand the necessity of obedience to God and to learn the doctrinal truths about salvation. They will respond easily to the necessity of growing in Christ and may become interested in encouraging others of their family and friends to become Christians. They need encouragement to daily devotions that include Scripture reading and prayer. They also need the very best example of Christianity that you as the teacher are able to set before them. Any hypocrisy on your part will be quickly detected by the student and irreparable damage may be done to his spiritual development.

As a teacher your life and the teachings of God's word will be under careful scrutiny by the whole class. Any failure or inconsistency on your part will be detected and exposed. "Take heed to yourself and to the doctrine. Continue in them, for in doing this you will save both yourself and those who hear you" (1 Tim. 4:16).

—Louis W. Garrett, Ph.D.

Notes

4:1

The Sermon on the Mount

Lesson 1

The Beatitudes (1)

With "Junior" students you are teaching a class that wants to be active. They are at the age of energy and doing things is much more profitable to them than listening to a lecture. If you want the student to "Turn You Off" in his mind the lecture is an excellent procedure to follow. Different age groups respond to different methods of teaching. Here are six different types of presentations to choose from in preparing for your classes.

- Storytelling
- Discussion
- Lecture
- Project-Research
- Question and Answer
- Recitation

It will be to your advantage to plan to use several of these in any one class and vary them from week to week. At the Junior age, they like to answer questions, hear a good Bible story told to them, recite what they have learned, and write down answers to questions you give verbally in class. This latter procedure is an excellent way to have a review of previous work or check on how well they have studied today's lesson.

In this quarter, we will be studying the Sermon on the Mount as recorded in Matthew 5-7. The scope of each lesson will be narrow as we study only a short section of this sermon each week. You will be teaching each student the kind of character the Lord wants him to have. To some teachers, this kind of lesson is not as easy to teach as one dealing with the story of a man's life. Many Old Testament stories are about people and may be easier to teach, but no lesson you teach will be more important than a lesson showing a student of this age *how to live.*

The first two lessons are on "The Beatitudes." Four are studied each week and should provide plenty of material with which to have good classes. One of the best ways to teach "Character Lessons" to students of this age is to transmit the characteristic being discussed to a live situation that the student might observe today. Meditate on the characteristic the verse speaks about and try to visualize a person with it. Then either make up a story or discuss a situation with the class where this was put into practice or was not put into practice in the life of someone. The students are to think about this in one of their thought questions at the end of the lesson. There are some good Old and New Testament stories of people that fit well some of these beatitudes.

The students can learn to quote these beatitudes without missing a word but the main test of whether the lesson is learned or not is whether they understand what they are saying. Can they put it into and make it a part of their life character. So work, not so much on what it says but what it means and help them make the application.

To give the student something to do in addition to the lesson for next class why not ask him to bring a picture to class which shows someone doing what one of these last four beatitudes teaches. It should not be difficult finding a picture of someone showing mercy, being a peacemaker, and possibly being persecuted for doing right. It will be interesting to see what he comes up with. Then have him interpret the picture for the class. This will show his understanding of the beatitude.

For this first class you might find pictures illustrating the teaching of the beatitudes. Show the pictures to the class one at a time, have some student tell you which beatitude it illustrates and discuss it. Now here is the first of a series of thirteen special tips.

Memory Work: Each lesson is preceded by a memory verse which

Special Tip Number 1

Always Go Into Your Classroom Prepared

Be sure you have studied your lesson; planned what you want to accomplish with the lesson, gathered your materials, decided upon your method of presentation, and know well your procedure when you get to class

applies to the lesson. Make these verses visible in the classroom, review them, have students look up the verses in their Bibles, and commit them to memory. A complete list of all memory verses for Lessons 1-13 are as follows:

Lesson 1: Matthew 5:3—"Blessed are the poor in spirit, For theirs is the kingdom of heaven."

Lesson 2: Matthew 5:7—"Blessed are the merciful, For they shall obtain mercy."

Lesson 3: Matthew 5:16—"Let your light so shine before men, that they may see your good works and glorify your Father in heaven."

Lesson 4: Matthew 5:20—"For I say to you, that unless your righteousness exceeds the righteousness of the scribes and Pharisees, you will by no means enter the kingdom of heaven."

Lesson 5: Matthew 5:22—"But I say to you that whoever is angry with his brother without a cause shall be in danger of the judgment. And whoever says to his brother, 'Raca!' shall be in danger of the council. But whoever says, 'You fool!' shall be in danger of hell fire."

Lesson 6: Matthew 5:37—"But let your 'Yes' be 'Yes,' and your 'No,' 'No.' For whatever is more than these is from the evil one."

Lesson 7: Matthew 5:44—"But I say to you, love your enemies, bless those who curse you, do good to those who hate you, and pray for those who spitefully use you and persecute you."

Lesson 8: Matthew 6:1—"Take heed that you do not do your charitable deeds before men, to be seen by them. Otherwise you have no reward from your Father in heaven."

Lesson 9: Matthew 6:9-11—"In this manner, therefore, pray: Our Father in heaven, Hallowed be Your name. Your kingdom come. Your will be done On earth as it is in heaven. Give us this day our daily bread."

Lesson 10: Matthew 6:33—"But seek first the kingdom of God and His righteousness, and all these things shall be added to you."

Notes

Notes

Lesson 11: Matthew 7:12—"Therefore, whatever you want men to do to you, do also to them, for this is the Law and the Prophets."

Lesson 12: Matthew 7:13-14—"Enter by the narrow gate; for wide is the gate and broad is the way that leads to destruction, and there are many who go in by it. "Because narrow is the gate and difficult is the way which leads to life, and there are few who find it."

Lesson 13: Matthew 7:21—"Not everyone who says to Me, 'Lord, Lord,' shall enter the kingdom of heaven, but he who does the will of My Father in heaven."

Bulletin Board Ideas:

Since the series of lessons deal with the Sermon on the Mount and character traits God expects each of us to have, begin a section on the bulletin board or wall called "Character Traits." Ask students during each lesson what character trait(s) the lesson is emphasizing and list those traits on your board or wall. If you have a digital camera, take pictures of each of your students and add them with their names to your board or wall so that they can see themselves developing the character traits discussed in each lesson.

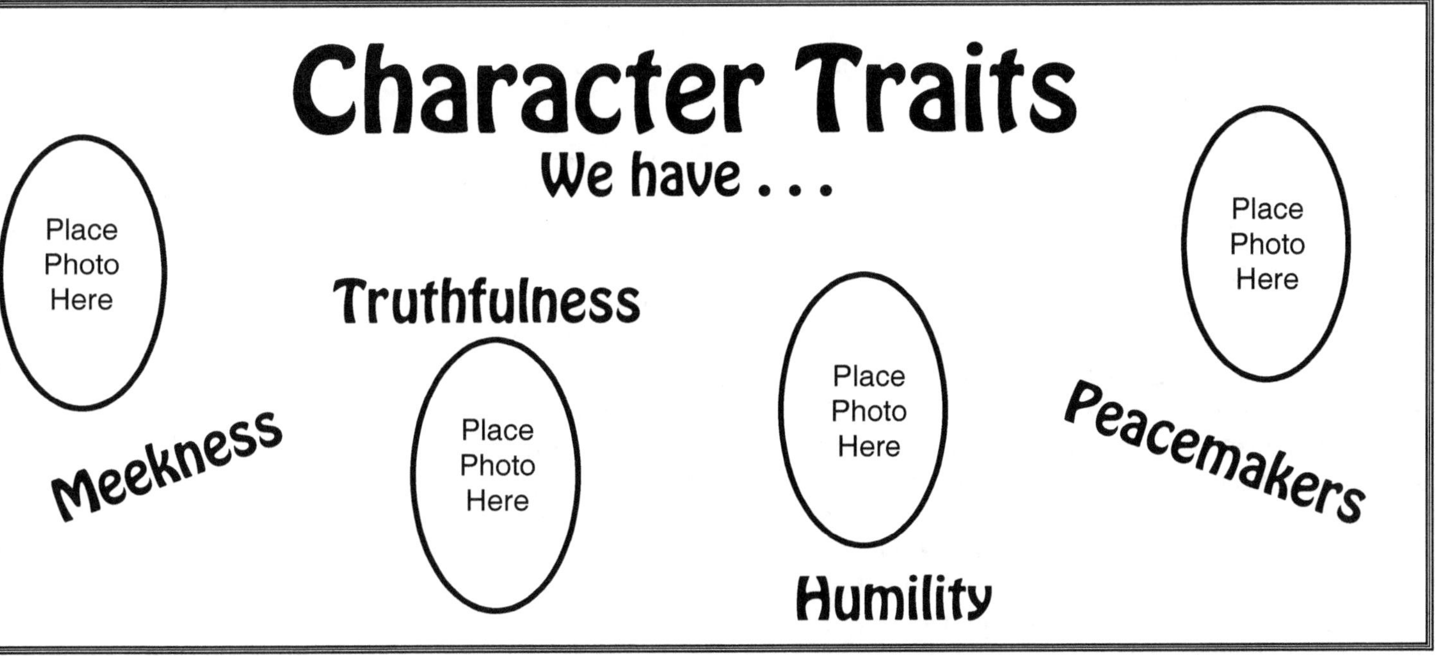

Use another section of the bulletin board (or another board if available) to dedicate to memory verses. You may title it any way you see fit; some suggestions might be: "We *Love* God's Word!," "Committed To Memory," "Verses To Know," etc. Type or write out each of the memory verses on a 4x6 index card, putting the scripture verse on one card and the corresponding scripture reference on another card. Place these on your bulletin board as you go through each lesson. You may then use the cards to review with, asking students to match the scripture verse with the scripture reference after 3-4 lessons have been taught. Mix up the cards and ask students to match them up with the correct scripture (see next page).

Another idea for memory work is to write or print out the memory verses in their entirety and post them on the bulletin board or wall.

We Love God's Word

Matt. 5:3-6	Blessed are the poor in spirit, For theirs is the kingdom of heaven. Blessed are those who mourn, For they shall be comforted. Blessed are the meek, For they shall inherit the earth. Blessed are those who hunger and thirst for righteousness, For they shall be filled.
Matt. 5:16	Let your light so shine before men, that they may see your good works and glorify your Father in heaven.
Matt. 5:20	For I say to you, that unless your righteousness exceeds the righteousness of the scribes and Pharisees, you will by no means enter the kingdom of heaven.

Challenge the students to commit each verse to memory. As they accomplish this, they may write their name or put a sticker on the verse (leave space when preparing the verses so that this can be done).

Additional Activities:

Reinforcing the content taught can be supplemented by an additional activity if time allows. Suggestions for additional activities which can be applied to the lessons are as follows:

Lesson 1: "This is YOUR life!"

Prepare 3x5 index cards with different life situations that apply to the age of students in your class, keeping in mind also the beatitudes which are being discussed in this lesson (humility, to mourn, meekness, hunger and thirst after righteousness). Place the cards in a hat or box, and allow students to draw a card, taking individual turns. Ask the student to read the situation and then discuss as a class the beatitude which could be applied. Ask students to prepare additional cards to add to the hat or box. (***Note To Teacher**: Preview the cards the students add before using them. Use good judgement as to which ones would be good to use and talk individually to students who are not serious about this assignment.)

Notes

Notes

Lesson 2

The Beatitudes (2)

Memory Verse: "Blessed are the merciful, For they shall obtain mercy" (Matt. 5:7).

This lesson is but a continuation of the last class and will be taught like that one. There are four separate thoughts contained in these last beatitudes and the time should be divided among them, giving you ten to fifteen minutes on each point.

Aim: The main objective is to get the pupils to understand the meaning of being merciful, pure in heart, a peacemaker and why they may have to take some persecution because of doing right. But, true understanding involves more than just being able to quote the memory verse. The lesson is of real value when they understand how to make the application to daily situations they face. Therefore, from your experience try to have real situations to tell them about where these four qualities were or were not applied. Everyone, especially children, seems to learn more quickly by being shown an example rather than by just telling them a truth.

In connection with the point on being pure in heart here is an experiment you can set up. Have a bowl of clear water and some food coloring. Explain that the clear water is pure because it is just water. Then let one of the students put a small amount of the food coloring into it. It is now no longer pure and in addition all the water has been affected by the small amount of coloring. After explaining the illustration, make the application to the mind or heart of the students and show how mixing even a small amount of color affects the water like small, sinful deeds affect the whole heart or mind and make God displeased.

In discussing the peacemaker role of God's children, get them to tell you and the class of a time when they did something that caused trouble and destroyed peace. Then have others tell of a time they tried to help bring about peace. Along with other areas where peacemaking is essential discuss the importance of racial peace which has always been a problem between races. Ephesians 2:14-16 is a perfect place to turn and read how God brought about a two-fold peace. Through Christ He broke down the wall of separation between Jew and Gentile and with the same sacrifice reconciled them both together unto God. The Law separated Jew and Gentile and Christ removed that. (Draw an end view of a wall with the words Jew and Gentile on each side of it. Then erase the wall, put Christ in its place and draw a large circle around all three.) (Then draw a second diagram with God written above and Jew and Gentile written side by side near the bottom of the chalkboard. Between write the letters S-I-N. This is what separates man from God. Now erase sin and put Christ in its place. Now draw a large circle around all four words showing that peace has been made.) This is an idea I use even when teaching adults. It is clear and easily seen even by children.

When discussing the beatitude of persecution two points can be made. (1) How men have been persecuted, as you read from the Bible and secular history, is interesting. (2) But, more important is why people have and still do today suffer for following God. It is the basic conflict between God and Satan, the conflict between good and evil, the conflict between Christians and those of the world. God rebukes sin through the Bible and through Christians. Those of the world have to oppose what is right in order to do their evil deeds. This makes for conflict and persecution. To be a child of God we must be ready to suffer when necessary.

"I've Got It!"

Prepare flashcards with a beatitude listed on one side only. Prepare another set of flashcards with the definition of each beatitude listed on one side only. Mix both sets of cards up and pass them out to the students. Students must work together to find the other classmate who has the card matching either the definition or the beatitude listed.

Special Tip Number 2

Maintaining Order

In teaching children, discipline must be maintained in the classroom. Among small children, order can be maintained by keeping them busy. Have a number of things to do. Among older children, keep them interested. They dislike lectures. They do like to be challenged and questioned; they like lively discussion. Discipline is a small problem when you keep their minds and/or bodies occupied with the lesson you have well prepared.

Notes

Notes

Lessons 3

Influence of Salt and Light

Memory Verse: "Let your light so shine before men, that they may see your good works and glorify your Father in heaven" (Matt. 5:16).

The lesson today is affirming that we all have an influence on others. It is not encouraging us to have an influence, but to have a *good* influence. So under the figures of a candle burning and salt that is good, Jesus discusses this subject.

The memory verse sums up the main point and no doubt in class there will be questions concerning "good works." If no one brings up this point, the teacher should bring it up for a lengthy discussion. Today we find many, even Christians, not knowing what "good works" are or how to know what the Lord considers "good works." The scripture that is most specific on this point is 2 Timothy 3:16, 17. After making this point stick with the class, then enumerate or get the students to point out some ways they can be busy with good works and have a good influence on those around them.

Experiment or Demonstration: Bring a candle to class. Help or have one of the students light it. Then have something you can put over it which the students cannot see through. Place it over the candle. Two things will happen: (1) No one will be able to see the light, and (2) the candle will soon go out. Point out that this is what happens to the person who is trying to cover up that he is trying to follow the Bible and God. Most of those in your class will not be Christians but some will become Christians during their junior years. In discussing these characteristics in any of the lessons I would not make it a point that these are things that Christians do, but these are the things a good person does or character traits of a person who is trying to please God. This of course will include all the Christians in the class, but it will not exclude those who may not yet have obeyed the gospel.

Other scriptures on the subject of light will be found in Acts 13:47; Romans 13:12; Ephesians 5:8; John 3:19-21. Under the three points on light, already pointed out in the student's book here, are scriptures to establish those points. Light . . .

1. Illuminates or makes known what is around it. John 3:19-21—Light shows up what is bad as well as what is good around it.
2. Guides those in its rays. Ps. 119:105—It is "a light unto my path."
3. Gives life to living things. John 1:4 speaks of life and light together as he speaks of it in a spiritual sense.

When discussing the salt of the earth have some of the students tell what most foods taste like when they have forgotten to salt it.

Whether it is light or salt, the value is the effect it has on other things. It is our duty and should be our pleasure to try to help others by showing them the right way. If the young people can learn early that others are watching as well as the Lord it will be a personal motivation to be more careful of their words and actions.

"Salt or Light?"

Ask students to brainstorm ways in which they can be salt or light as discussed in the lesson. Challenge them to come up with a class list of ten examples. Once they reach ten, challenge them to list twenty. Post the list in the classroom so that each time you meet together you can ask the students in what way were they salt or light since you last saw them. Add those to your list and continue building the class through this entire set of lessons.

Special Tip Number 3

Avoid Discomfort, Disturbance and Distraction

These are three of your worst enemies and can completely nullify the effects of a well prepared lesson. See to it that you have a comfortable and quiet room in which to study with your students.

Notes

Notes

Lesson 4

Jesus and the Law

Memory Verse: "For I say to you, that unless your righteousness exceeds the righteousness of the scribes and Pharisees, you will by no means enter the kingdom of heaven" (Matt. 5:20).

This lesson is easily separated into two sections for the purpose of teaching the class. However, it is all one thought when viewed from the position of Christ.

Verses 17 and 18 are easily studied together and contain one main thought. Christ came to teach and fulfill. Much of what the Jews had been taught about the law and the prophets by the Pharisees was different from what He was going to say about it. Since He was new on the scene, some might begin thinking that He wanted to destroy the law because what He said about the law often sounded foreign to what the Pharisees were saying. Somebody was destroying the truth of the law without a doubt, but it was not Christ.

Verse 19 is a description of one thing the Pharisees and scribes had done to the Old Testament. They had divided the laws into two groups: those which were least in importance and the consequences were minor if they were broken; and those which were greater and more important. Jesus was emphasizing that the Pharisees were wrong in this and that not even a jot or tittle would be removed from any of the law until it was fulfilled by Him.

This raised a question concerning the righteousness of the Pharisees. If they were wrong in doing this, they could be wrong in many things. At this point Jesus has had little contact with these men since this is early in His ministry. But, He knows what they are like. Here He does not discuss the qualities of their righteousness but simply states that it meets with God's disapproval. You have to go to other places to see what it is like. Matthew 15 and 23 are two good sections to learn more of their disposition. Four points are made in the student lesson. You may use these and find others to discuss with your class.

Galatians 3:15-29 is a good place to do more study on the purpose of the law in the Old Testament. Paul there says the Law was to bring the Jews to Christ that they might be justified by faith in Him. God always intended that Christ would end the Old Testament and His life would fulfill it.

A Possible Problem: Knowing Christ said that He did not come to destroy the law and also knowing Colossians 2:14 shows He did take it away or "abolish" it (Eph. 2:15), we may have a potential problem in understanding both these scriptures. If the problem arises in class here is the solution. In Ephesians 2:15, Romans 7:6, and 2 Corinthians 3:7, 11, 13, 14 the word "abolish" is translated from a word meaning, "to render idle, unemployed, inactive, inoperative. . ." (Thayer's, *Greek English Lexicon*). The word used in Matthew 5:17 is a different word meaning, "to dissolve, disunite. . . demolish." This word is never used in connection with the removal of the Law of Moses. It is one thing to take fire to a law book and burn it up, thus dissolving, disuniting, demolishing it. It is another thing to close the book, place it on a shelf, and abolish the force of its laws. The law of Moses still has some use (Rom. 15:14; 1 Cor. 10:11), though not as a law to guide us today. Christ abolished the legal authority and force of its laws but He did not demolish and dissolve them. They are still with us.

Notes

Things to do: Show how prophecy is fulfilled by taking one or more of the prophecies of Christ and show its fulfillment. In the gospels, five specific prophecies are fulfilled in Christ while he is young. Juniors might be more interested in discussing these. Here are the scriptures:

Matt. 1:23 — **Isa. 7:14**
Matt. 2:6 — **Mic. 5:2**
Matt. 2:15 — **Hos. 11:1**
Matt. 2:18 — **Jer. 31:15**
Matt. 2:23 — **Isa. 11:1** in the Hebrew. You may want to omit this one from discussion.

Jesus fulfilled many prophecies like these in His short lifetime.

Something else you can do is draw a perpendicular line on the board with a heading on each side. At the top on the left side of the line write, "The Pharisees' Righteousness." On the other side write, "Our Righteousness." List the Pharisee's characteristics first then the opposite of these on the other side. Let different students help you figure out what to put on "Our" side. More "tips" next time.

Special Tip Number 4

In Your Class Preparation Let Your Bible Be First

All other sources of materials and information must take a secondary place in your study. Know what the Bible says and go from there.

"Sword Drill!"

The Bible is our best defense against Satan, and we can use it as our "sword" to fight off sin by knowing what God"s Word contains. This activity helps students remember where to locate books of the Bible.

Ask students to close their Bibles. You choose a book of the Bible, tell it to the students, and once you say, Go!", students may look up that book as fast as they can. Ask students to close their Bibles again, give them another book to look up, and say "Go!" You may keep a tally of points if you wish as a challenge for the students to see who finds the book the fastest. Once they are familiar with the books of the Bible, you may ask them to look up individual scripture verses referred to in the lessons. The first student who finds the verse, may read it. You may use this activity in subsequent lessons. Students will learn that when you announce "Sword Drill!", they are to close their Bibles and prepare to find what you choose to have them look up. If you have students who are consistently the first ones to find the verses, pair them up with a student who needs help in this area and work as teams, keeping points again to see which team finds it first.

Notes

Lesson 5

Anger and Lust

Memory Verse: "But I say to you that whoever is angry with his brother without a cause shall be in danger of the judgment. And whoever says to his brother, 'Raca!' shall be in danger of the council. But whoever says, 'You fool!' shall be in danger of hell fire" (Matt. 5:22).

By the time a student has reached the age of your pupils, he has had some personal experience with anger. However, there will be some things about anger that he will not understand. In this lesson you want to analyze anger and study it from a practical point of view.

You might begin your class by having a brainstorming session. Have the students tell some of the things that make them angry. Now what is there about the situation that can justify or at least cause the anger? Most all cases of anger are caused by three conditions of mind or body: *mistreatment*, *disappointment,* or *disapproval.* You might write these three words on the board beside one another and list the specific examples of anger given by the students under the appropriate column. This can help the student to see what really causes one to become angry. Likely, most of what causes anger in one student may be grouped under one heading. This will show something of his basic nature.

Here is another suggestion. There are many scriptures on anger in the Bible. Take several of these and look at the results of anger. Examples:

Proverbs 14:17—does foolish things

Proverbs 29:22—stirs up strife (See Prov. 15:18)

Luke 15:28— anger caused the older brother to pout and refuse to be reconciled to his lost brother. He *disapproved* of the way he had been treated. Tell the class this story and discuss the anger of the older brother.

Lust

This is not an easy subject to discuss with juniors and get them to understand. Likely they will be interested in the subject of divorce, however, and that is important for them to understand. Most of your time might be spent on this part of this major section of your lesson.

One point of emphasis underlies the subject of both anger and lust in today's lesson. That is the emphasis Christ places upon our thinking, feeling, and keeping our hearts right. If the young people can see this truth and, with your help, get some experience putting this into practice we will have helped them very much. This is the point of emphasis. Sins of the mind are as wrong before God and Christ as sins of outward action.

Another passage on the subject of fornication and adultery in connection with divorce is found in Matthew 19:2. The chain of events leading to divorce might be viewed in this order:

Lust in the Heart **Adultery** **Divorce**

Notes

The lesson today is very important in laying a good foundation on proper attitudes of a Christian. Prepare well your class and have a good one.

Use class time in lessons 5 and 6 to review previous lessons since you are about halfway through the series. Choose any of the activities suggested for lessons 1-4 to use as review activities. Keep working on memory verses!

Special Tip Number 5

Before You Accept the Responsibility of Teaching a Class: Desire to Teach

A teacher who teaches a class because he feels like he has to and not because he wants to seldom prepares adequately. Neither will he have and show the interest necessary to be a good teacher.

Notes

Lesson 6

Letting Your Word Count

Memory Verse: "But let your 'Yes' be 'Yes,' and your 'No,' 'No.' For whatever is more than these is from the evil one" (Matt. 5:37).

It seems that swearing has always played a role of confirmation in man's dealing with man. In Hebrews 6:16 this is affirmed by God. But in this lesson, Jesus shows a different attitude His people are to take toward swearing.

He approaches the subject from a negative and from a positive point of view. If you teach it this way, it might be easier for the pupils to understand and will be some variety from the approach taken in the pupil's workbook.

In verses 34-36 we have the negative discussion and it is simply, "Swear not at all." Whether the students understand all the reasons behind this prohibition will in no way affect their clear understanding of this plain prohibition. The Jews understood they were not to swear falsely (forswear), but there were a number of objects God permitted them to swear by, they thought. Christ mentioned several things people swore by and there were doubtless many more. But, Jesus said for them not to swear at all. You will notice in James 5:12 the same prohibition. It will be interesting to parallel these two scriptures, Matthew 5:34-37 and James 5:12. You need not copy all the verses but the words that are alike.

Question the Student: Now get the students to tell the class some of the swearing they hear among their classmates. Perhaps in the past they have done this themselves. See if they will tell the class some of the statements used in confirming a statement.

But, the most important consideration in this lesson is the positive statement of Christ in verse 37. See also the last part of James 5:12.

Those who follow Christ will always mean what they say. They are as good as their word and their word is always to be true. Why should we not swear at all? You might list these on the chalkboard.

1. Jesus said not to swear. (That would be sufficient if no other reason existed.)
2. No purpose is served by a Christian swearing. (His word is to be true because he is a Christian.)
3. Jesus says it is of evil.

Look at some of the evils connected with swearing. To swear concerning a statement is accepted as proof that the statement is true by many men. So if a person really wants to tell a lie and have it believed he can just swear by it and more people will believe it. Swearing is just an added tool of deception.

Swearing serves no good purpose because, if something is true, it is true without swearing. If it is false, swearing only adds to the deception. If a person has a reputation for being untruthful, swearing will not help his words. If a person has a reputation for being truthful, his words need no help.

Some student may ask about swearing in the court room. Among Christians there are divided sentiments on this point. Albert Barnes has some thoughtful comments on this point if you have access to his commentaries. In our courts, which receive testimony daily from a cross section of our society made up mainly of those who do not follow Christ, it is necessary to compel witnesses to take the oath of truth. This gives legal grounds to prosecute and punish one who would lie on the witness stand. Our courts would be in shambles without it, since so many feel little guilt about lying and could easily be bribed to lie. In Matthew 5 and James 5 it does not seem to me Jesus was discussing the judicial oath of our courts but in our daily conversation where the oath really serves no purpose and has no penalties to enforce truthfulness.

The main lesson Jesus seems to be emphasizing is this: Because of what we are, we will tell the truth and be reliable in our words.

If you have extra time in this lesson, review the memory verse last week and see how many remember the "Beatitudes".

Remember that review always pays. It is time well spent.

Special Tip Number 6

When You Enter The Classroom Know What You Are Going To Do. Know Your Teaching Procedure

Not only do you need to have a good knowledge of your material, you also must know your teaching procedure for the day.

Notes

Notes

Lesson 7

My Treatment of Others

Memory Verse: "But I say to you, love your enemies, bless those who curse you, do good to those who hate you, and pray for those who spitefully use you and persecute you" (Matt. 5:44).

The lesson today will probably be one of the hardest ones to put into practice of all you will study. The truth of the lesson is easy to understand and all of us can see why it is the best course to follow. It has been said that Matthew 5:39 is the hardest verse in the Bible to obey. Perhaps it is for many people and likely will be for your pupils in the days ahead. So how do you prepare that student to obey in life the truth he learns in mind through this lesson? When you enter the classroom this week, that will be the job you face.

I believe the best approach we have is that used by Christ in Matthew 5:45-48. He showed *motives* for doing what He had just taught. Let me suggest that you emphasize these and thoroughly discuss them during most of your class period. Here they are:

1. To be children of God—He does good to the just and unjust.
2. We are no better than anyone else if we are good only to those who are good to us. Ask the students if they want to be no better than those who wrong them.
3. What reward is there for doing good to those who are good to us and bad to those who do us wrong?
4. The great motive is to be perfect as our Father in heaven is perfect.
5. Not listed in the text of Matthew 5 but very good is a review of how Christ lived among men and did good to those who hated Him, even dying for them.

There is plenty of material here to last most of the class.

If time is available, study the specific rules Christ gave to guide us in our relationship with those who wrong us. Discuss them one at a time. The students have three questions at the end of their lesson for thought and discussion. Spend some time with them, thinking of situations they have been in where they needed to apply today's lesson.

The real test to them will not be whether they know what to do but will they have the courage and motivation to do what is right in the real situation when it arises. One problem they may have at this age is understanding what a personal enemy is. Children have few of them since it is so easy to forgive and forget at that age. They likely do not know enemies as they might some day.

No lesson in this quarter will be more important than this one. Pray about it, think about it, and plan well for it. There is much material with which to work and it is not difficult to teach. Have a good class and hope you can implant a seed in their minds that each pupil will bless you for in days to come.

"Challenge Activity"

Challenge students to think of ways they can help someone or treat someone better than they have in the past. Provide paper and pencils so students can write down what they have thought of, and ask them to take action on it before the next class time. Ask them to also write down how the other person responded. Prepare to discuss these scenarios with the students during the next class time. They may have received a variety of responses and some may not have been positive.

Special Tip Number 7

Always Prepare Your Lessons With the Age Level and Needs of Your Students in Mind

It is sometimes helpful to pick out one of your students in your mind and prepare the lesson specifically for that person. It will help personalize your material more.

Notes

Notes

Lesson 8

Alms – Prayer – Fasting

Memory Verse: "Take heed that you do not do your charitable deeds before men, to be seen by them. Otherwise you have no reward from your Father in heaven" (Matt. 6:1).

Be Ready for Questions

In the preparation of these lessons, it is not possible to cover all points of the Bible text. Since the students will read all the text they will likely have questions not covered in their workbook. The teacher needs to be aware of this and *anticipate student questions.*

In this lesson, one question that may be asked, but which needs to be explained anyway, is taken from the memory verse. The memory verse in the lesson is from the ASV. The KJV has "alms" where the ASV has "righteousness." The latter is more correct when the many manuscripts are studied that were not available to the translators of the KJV. Also, from the context, it is more correct in meaning with the alms, prayers, and fasting illustrations of a man's righteousness. Righteousness is a state of being which exists when that which is right has been done.

It also will be a good idea to be ready to discuss "fasting" with the class and a good Bible dictionary will be helpful here. It basically is abstinence from food or certain foods usually for religious purposes.

The Lesson to Get

There is one major point made in the lesson today as is usually true of each lesson. It is stated in the memory verse. When a Christian serves God acceptably, it must be with sincerity, directed to God for His glory, and for our divine reward. Drill this lesson into the students' minds with numerous illustrations. Use things we do today in worship and in being helpful to others. Our motive in doing what God said should always be because God said it and not to please others. Illustrate with singing, praying, giving, or teaching. Do not do these things so others will think well of you or brag on your singing, praying, etc. This is the lesson.

Here is a suggestion about procedure in teaching the lesson. After attendance and other preliminary steps have been taken plan to discuss the three points: alms, prayer, and fasting. During the discussion have the students pick out the things that are similar in each case; "they have their reward" and "are hypocrites." You may only lightly touch the prayer of the Lord since that will be discussed more thoroughly next week.

After studying these illustrations of Christ, get the class to come up with the common lesson in each. If they can grasp this, it will enforce their confidence in being able to understand the Bible for themselves. This is a lesson many adults still need to know. Finally go over the lesson answers they have in their books and help each find his grade.

“Memory Match”

This activity focuses on memory verses. Using the cards on your bulletin board, take them down, mix them up, and pass them out to students (this can be managed much the same way as the activity suggested in Lesson 2: “I’ve Got It!”). Pass the cards out to students and allow them to work together to match the verses with the correct scripture reference. Ask one or two students to look up the verses to make sure the matches are correct.

Notes

Special Tip Number 8

When You Prepare and Teach a Lesson, Teach It to Meet Today’s Needs and Show How to Use the Lesson Daily

It is easy to cover good lessons and very important material but leave the application in the first century. Let the student see the Bible speaking to him *today*.

Notes

Lesson 9

The Prayer Christ Taught

Memory Verse: "In this manner, therefore, pray: Our Father in heaven, Hallowed be Your name. Your kingdom come. Your will be done On earth as it is in heaven. Give us this day our daily bread" (Matt. 6:9-11).

The prayer Christ taught His disciples to pray contains a brief outline of those things God wants to see His disciples concerned about. He wants to see us so interested in them, that we will want to talk to Him about them.

An Exercise: At the beginning of the class tell the students you want him to think of something he has heard others pray for or about. Give them a few minutes to think. You might check the roll while they do this. As you ask them for their answers, write them in brief form on the board. You may be able to go around the class two times since they may think of many things. This will likely prove as interesting to you as to them. For your own help in knowing what to emphasize in the class, also do this yourself. See if you can recall things you have prayed for or heard others pray for that they did not mention. It would be good to emphasize those things that are scriptural which they did not recall. This should get the class off to a good start.

Before studying the text point by point, this would likely be the best time to drill and check the class on the memory verse. Be sure they know it well and have it fresh upon their minds.

Now you are ready to cover the Bible text, verse by verse, as time permits. Get them to think and express themselves. You might try reading the different statements, one by one, and get them to discuss, ask questions, and give the meaning of each.

1. Our Father which art in heaven, Hallowed be thy name.
2. Thy will be done in earth as it is in heaven.
3. Give us this day our daily bread.
4. Forgive us our debts, as we forgive our debtors.
5. Lead us not into temptation but deliver us from evil.
6. For thine is the kingdom, and the power, and the glory, for ever, Amen.

This prayer does not include everything for which we may pray and the children will know of things they pray for that may not be mentioned, but this is a good place to begin doing some very important teaching on prayer and more teaching needs to be done on this subject.

There was one thing Christ proceeded to further explain after the prayer was concluded and that was point 4 above about forgiveness. One condition of forgiveness before God often overlooked is clearly emphasized here. God will not forgive us unless and until we have forgiven those who may have sinned against us. To be forgiven we must be willing to forgive. Why would we expect God to forgive us if we would not forgive others? This may be discussed at the time you discuss number 4 above.

Notes

The word "debt," in the lesson today means, "that which is legally due," when it is used literally. In the lesson, it is used figuratively with the same idea. It is, "sin as a debt, because it demands expiation, and thus payment by way of punishment, Matt. 6:12" (definitions from W. E. Vine, *Expository Dictionary of New Testament Words*). Have a good class.

"Powerful Prayer"

In this activity, you will ask the students to write a prayer, using the lesson as a guide. Ask for volunteers to read their prayers to the class or post the prayers on a wall or bulletin board. You may also wish to provide a spiral bound notebook to each student, so that they may begin to write and develop their prayers. Sometimes it is easier for students of this age to write down their thoughts, than to express them verbally for fear of embarrassment in front of their classmates.

Special Tip Number 9

A Teacher Must Always Be Aware of What He Is Trying to Do for the Student to Meet His Needs

You are trying to stimulate his thinking; motivate his actions to do what is right and increase his appreciation for fhe Bible and what God has done.

Notes

Lesson 10

Learning True Value

Memory Verse: "But seek first the kingdom of God and His righteousness, and all these things shall be added to you" (Matt. 6:33).

There is too much material in the Bible text today to cover it all in the student's book. Therefore it will be up to you, the teacher, to fill in some of the details from the Bible.

The approach taken in the student's lesson is to pick out three important principles mentioned by Christ and elaborate on them. This is the skeleton around which you can build.

In the June, 1969, issue of the *National Geographic,* there was an interesting article on a treasure hunt undertaken in the sea off the coast of Ireland. It told of treasures found from one of the ships of the Spanish Armada. In more recent years, treasure hunters have located the Titanic and several other ships off the coasts of the United States and several foreign countries.

As a brain tester you might have the class think of some of the things that make a treasure valuable. Any treasure that is a real treasure is, first of all, worth very much. It is of value or it is no treasure.

Second, the lasting quality is important. That which lasts only a short time is usually of less value than that which lasts a long time.

Something else to consider is this: for anything to be a treasure to you it is necessary to "hold on to it." And how safe your treasure is will depend on where you keep it. Jesus seems to be emphasizing the supreme importance of laboring for the treasure that can be stored in heaven, that will last forever, and that is of the greatest value.

With our life, we will have *time*, *abilities*, and *money*. In this lesson Jesus wants to direct all three of these in the direction of God and He concludes with this admonition in verse 33.

The treasure is simply this: it is what we accumulate before God to our credit as a result of putting His word and way first in our lives.

If He does not come first in all our considerations, then a way that is not His comes first. When we have the choice, we usually put first what we love most or most love to do. That is why our heart is where our treasure or first interest is.

In first century times, men sometimes tried to steal another's treasures. The same is true in the lesson today. There are two enemies mentioned by Christ.

One is in verse 24. Read it and see if the class can find it. It is simply dividing our interests and service. Under no condition does God accept a divided service. All that we do is to be done in a way He will approve and be pleased with.

Growing out of this is a symptom of trouble. Anxiety and worry about the provisions and needs of this life can easily betray an interest that is physical and not spiritual. The last part of the chapter shows God will see we are provided for, if we put Him first. In 2 Thessalonians 3:12 we are shown to work for our daily needs and Matthew 6:11 shows God wants us to pray to Him for them. If we will trust Him, work, and pray, we will be provided for.

Notes

Regardless to what happens, we are to put obedience to God's will first. Oppose the two enemies of this: divided interest and anxiety over food, shelter, and clothing. Trust God and continue to lay up those treasures in heaven. These are some of the things I would cover and they can be arranged a number of ways. You choose how to arrange them and have a good class. Here is tip number 10.

Special Tip Number 10

To Have a Successful and Enjoyable Class The Teacher Must Be Able to Gain and Hold the Attention of the Students

Here are four suggestions:

- Always be prepared
- Vary your presentation
- Use a variety of materials
- Do not overlook the importance of being enthusiastic

Again, take this opportunity to review previous lessons and to use one of the other activities. Continue "Sword Drill" and memory verse work.

Notes

Lesson 11

The Golden Rule

Memory Verse: "Therefore, whatever you want men to do to you, do also to them, for this is the Law and the Prophets" (Matt. 7:12).

The main emphasis in the lesson today is on the memory verse and what is commonly called the Golden Rule. Verses 1-12 cover much more than that and you can cover as much of this as time permits. However, because of the importance of Matthew 7:12 to the life of each pupil for as long as he lives, spend most of the time here.

Under the heading, "Let's Talk" in the student's work, there are five thought questions. These questions will give you considerable latitude in broadening the discussion and making numerous applications. Question two will be especially good for discussion. Look for reasons why the Golden Rule is best. Here are some suggestions for thought.

- Best for us because it is obedience to God. If there was no other reason this would be sufficient to the Christian and young person seeking to please God.
- It may encourage someone who would do you wrong to refrain. See Romans 12:20.
- If we want good done to us (and who does not), we can be assured others do also, so it will be showing others what you like.
- It will discourage retaliation for any wrong done others because, if you do them good, there is no need or cause to "get back" at you.

Sometime during class have the students tell you which rules Christ broke with His law and which one He wants enforced. The class will remember this.

On the first part of the lesson from the Bible, there is a discussion of the judgment made by one person on the actions of another. The point of the lesson is a condemnation of hypocritical judgment. He is not saying we are not to correct others when they are wrong or point out error when we see it. Nor is he saying we can say nothing to another unless we have a life that is stronger and one with fewer weakness than another. This would be most difficult, if not impossible, to know. He is speaking of the hypocritical fault finder who does nothing to clean up his own life. In verse 5 he is called a hypocrite so we know these comments are true of the critical character.

Sometimes people are critical of others just to cover up their own weaknesses and failures. At other times the hypocrite may be critical of one who sought to correct his hypocritical ways. It is just a way of "getting back" at the better person.

By the time you have covered this material and the five discussion questions, class will likely be over. However, if you have a few more minutes verses 7-11 still have not been discussed. Here is the assurance of God that He not only knows how to give what we need but also is able and willing, if we will come to Him asking for what we need.

Notes

Another lesson in connection with the memory verse is this: if we know how to give good things to others and do good things for others we should do it. Do to them the good things you would want them to do to you. Now, here is your special tip this week.

Special Tip Number 11

When You Drill on Memory Work Keep in Mind the Real Value Has Come When They Understand and Explain What They Have Memorized

Too often we let the memory verse be the end of it. A child can memorize almost anything without understanding all of it. Remember this.

Use this lesson to brainstorm ways in which they would like to be treated. Challenge them again to take action on the lessons learned in this lesson and write them down or share with the class what they did.

Notes

Lesson 12

The Two Ways

Memory Verse: "Enter by the narrow gate; for wide is the gate and broad is the way that leads to destruction, and there are many who go in by it. Because narrow is the gate and difficult is the way which leads to life, and there are few who find it" (Matt. 7:13-14).

There are only two more lessons this quarter and, apart from the study of this specific lesson, I would plan to have a review of the first lessons (perhaps six of them) today. Even if the students cannot recall exactly what the memory verses say, see that they do understand their meaning. Plan a good review with two or three good questions on each lesson. Have your preparation for this review ready ahead of time and plan at least 15 or 20 minutes for this.

With the remainder of the time, you will be discussing Gates, Ways, and Destinations. Above all you will be studying what is involved when a person decides which gate he will enter.

After reviewing the memory verse with the students, you might begin with this most important question. Does God force anyone to enter a particular gate? The answer is, of course, no. Next question: Then who determines which gate you enter? Each individual decides for himself. As a result of this the destination reached at the end of the way is also determined by our choice and God is not to blame if we make the wrong choice.

Word groupings are interesting to work with on the chalkboard and in this lesson there are two groups that are automatically forced together:

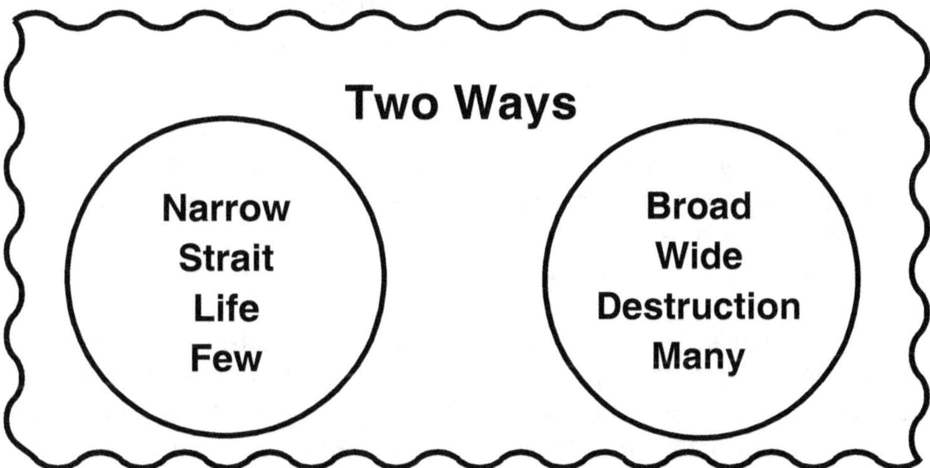

For discussion and class participation you might begin by writing the words, "Narrow" and "Broad" on opposite sides of the board. Then see if someone in the class can give you two more opposites and continue until all the words are grouped together. Now you are ready for the lesson: you cannot follow the broad way with the many and have life with the few. When the student chooses, or anyone chooses, the choice is made and all go together. Emphasize that, if they decide to enter the wide gate which is the gate entered by those who do not obey the gospel and who choose not to follow God, the end will be destruction. Discuss Hell; its nature, duration, inhabitants, and some of the things God says about it.

Notes

Then show what a difference it makes to be wise and do as Christ says, choosing the narrow gate. How much happier now and in eternity are those who choose life over death and destruction. Discuss Heaven as you did Hell.

This is a good time to discuss the gospel and what is involved in obeying it. At this age (the beginning of the junior studies), likely none is in need of obeying the gospel. I would point this out and indicate who needs to obey the gospel. Between the ages of 9 and 12, children often become frightened, having heard about baptism all their lives and its necessity, and yet not having been baptized. They can understand what baptism is and its purpose long before they become aware of sin and the need to obey Him. While pointing this out to them, it still is a good time and place to discuss the gospel objectively, so they will understand what to do when they are old enough. "Strait" does not mean difficult so much as it means "narrow," as hemmed in like a narrow gorge between rocks, as one explained it. It is a way with controls, directions, instructions. If followed with faithfulness, they lead to life.

With the remaining time, emphasize the fact that not everyone teaches the truth as is seen in verses 15-20. These men sometimes keep otherwise good people off the strait way by their false doctrines.

This should be a busy day with plenty to do. Final suggestions coming up next week. Here is special tip number 12.

Special Tip Number 12

Review Is One of the Most Important Tools of Learning. Never Overlook The Power It Has for You and the Pupil

It helps reinforce what has been covered in a lesson; it helps you see what they have learned and have not learned; it helps you correct wrong impressions they may have previously gained that you were unaware of. Review often.

Review, review, review! Students of this age need reinforcement of the lessons taught in this series as they develop the character traits God expects of us. Review the character traits taught at the beginning of this series and ask students what they have learned during this series of lessons. Their answers can be very insightful! Continue to help them develop, as pre-teens, the love of God's word and how they can strive to be a Christian.

Notes

Lesson 13

The Two Buiders

Memory Verse: "Not everyone who says to Me, 'Lord, Lord,' shall enter the kingdom of heaven, but he who does the will of My Father in heaven" (Matt. 7:21).

Since you are completing the book with this lesson, make plans as you did last week to review lessons 7-12 for about 15-20 minutes. Review the memory work for meaning and understanding more than for exact quotations. This can be most valuable to the students.

With this lesson you and the students who have been with you for thirteen weeks come to the end of the Sermon on the Mount. Jesus has completed giving, in very brief form, some of the most important lessons we will ever learn. Yet they are presented in such a way that they are easy to learn and even memorize. In fact this was the first section of the Bible including several chapters that I ever memorized. This sermon did not concern itself with specific acts of obedience and service as much as it did with the heart, the feelings, the attitudes, the values, and principles upon which to build the full and good life. It is impossible to sit at the feet of Jesus and hear Him preach this sermon without coming away moved and determined to be a better person.

If you and each student in your class have gained a greater appreciation of Jesus from these lessons the time all of us have spent has been well rewarded.

It is fitting that Jesus would conclude this sermon with a firm warning against just learning without doing.

The religion Christ came to instill in those who would be His disciples involves action and obedience. His lessons are all for *doing* not just knowing. Let this be point number one you emphasize to your class this final lesson. They all know the song and story of the two builders. Now it is your privilege to really impress upon them what it means to each of them personally.

Do this by reviewing different instructions Christ has given in this sermon and which the students have learned. When they tell you the truth concerning what Christ taught is to be done, ask them then how the lesson today would apply to that point. The lesson with which we are concluding ties directly to every lesson we have studied.

As the lesson is presented by Christ, He states the principle of truth in verses 21-23. Then He clearly illustrates with the two builders what He meant.

To avoid separation from God it is not enough to:

- Claim you are doing good works
- Call on the name of the Lord
- Be busy doing religious things

The only thing that matters to Christ and the only thing He will take into account in judgment is this: ***Have I done the sayings of Christ or the teaching of Christ?***

Notes

Jesus talked about building two houses. Both men were busy and active with their work. The work of one was wasted and the work of the other rewarded and lasting. What is the difference? Ask the students. Maybe some of the boys have seen the footing poured for a solid footing and foundation to a house. Maybe some can tell about building experiences they have had.

The difference in standing and falling is simple to see. If we know and do, we stand. If we know and do not, we fall and great will be the fall.

Encourage each pupil to put into practice every day what he has learned that Jesus wants him to do. Do not wait until later. Tell them to begin doing it now.

And so we conclude thirteen weeks of working together to try and put into the minds of young people lessons they must learn and never forget. Though we have been trying to teach them, I have a good feeling both of us have likely learned more than they. This is one of the many advantages we have when we try to be good teachers.

Here is the final special tip and, though last in number, it is perhaps first in importance. I have hoped these Special Tips would concentrate on points which need our weekly and determined attention if we are to do our best.

Special Tip Number 13

Every Teacher Must Set an Example Before the Students at All Times of What Jesus Would Have Him Be

Unfaithfulness to Christ outside the classroom can destroy the teacher's influence in the classroom and start a student on the road to hypocrisy and final destruction. Show them how to do faithfully what they study and learn with you in their classes.

4:2

Leaders in Israel

Lesson 1

Abraham – The Friend of God

Introduction to the Quarter

Memory Work: Each lesson is preceded by a memory verse which applies to the lesson. Make these verses visible in the classroom, review them, have students look up the verses in their Bibles, and commit them to memory. A complete list of all memory verses for Lessons 1-13 are as follows:

- Lesson 1: Romans 4:20—"He did not waver at the promise of God through unbelief, but was strengthened in faith, giving glory to God."
- Lesson 2: Acts 3:22—"For Moses truly said to the fathers, 'The Lord your God will raise up for you a Prophet like me from your brethren. Him you shall hear in all things, whatever He says to you."
- Lesson 3: Hebrews 4:16—"Let us therefore come boldly to the throne of grace, that we may obtain mercy and find grace to help in time of need."
- Lesson 4: Joshua 1:9—"Have I not commanded you? Be strong and of good courage; do not be afraid, nor be dismayed, for the Lord your God is with you wherever you go."
- Lesson 5: Judges 6:12—"And the Angel of the Lord appeared to him, and said to him, "The Lord is with you, you mighty man of valor!"
- Lesson 6: Galatians 6:1—"Brethren, if a man is overtaken in any trespass, you who are spiritual restore such a one in a spirit of gentleness, considering yourself lest you also be tempted."
- Lesson 7: Matthew 5:44—"But I say to you, love your enemies, bless those who curse you, do good to those who hate you, and pray for those who spitefully use you and persecute you."
- Lesson 8: Hebrew 13:6—"So we say with confidence, 'The Lord is my helper; I will not fear. What can man do to me?'"
- Lesson 9: Psalm 28:7—"The Lord is my strength and my shield; My heart trusts in Him, and I am helped; Therefore my heart greatly rejoices, And with my song I will praise Him."
- Lesson 10: I Thessalonians 5:8-9—"But let us who are of the day be sober, putting on the breastplate of faith and love, and as a helmet the hope of salvation. For God did not appoint us to wrath, but to obtain salvation through our Lord Jesus Christ,"
- Lesson 11: John 15:13—"Greater love has no one than this, than to lay down one's life for his friends."
- Lesson 12: Ezra 7:10—"For Ezra had prepared his heart to seek the Law of the Lord, and to do it, and to teach statutes and ordinances in Israel."
- Lesson 13: I Corinthinans 16:13—"Watch, stand fast in the faith, be brave, be strong."

BULLETIN BOARD IDEAS: Since this series of lessons deal with leaders or heroes of the Bible, a bulletin board dedicated to "Heroes of the Bible" would be appropriate. List each name of the leader from each lesson (Abraham, Moses, Aaron, etc.) and this will help the children remember these great leaders from the Bible. Another bulletin board or section of a wall can be dedicated to Memory Verses and each memory verse can be printed out and placed in this section of the room.

Notes

Heroes of the Bible

Abraham	Gideon	Jeremiah
Moses	Samuel	Esther
Aaron	David	Ezra
Joshua	Elijah	Nehemiah
	Isaiah	

SUPPLEMENTAL ACTIVITIES: There is a great deal of good material covered in each of these lessons, therefore supplemental activities will not be offered for each lesson. Maps of Israel, a Bible dictionary, Bible concordance (or even a computer Bible program), and Bibles for the students to use will be useful for this series of lessons. Modern day pictures of Israel can also be useful for students so that they can apply the lessons in today's world and current events. As you teach three or four lessons, an activity such as "Who Am I?" would be a good review activity (see below for instructions). Continue to work and review memory verses each week and discuss with students how they can be applied in their personal lives at home and at school. Each of the lessons discuss character traits which can be developed in children of this age group, so it will be important to stress within each lesson the character trait the children observe of Abraham, Moses, and so on.

Who Am I?

This activity reviews the events and character traits displayed by the people studied in this series of lessons. In the first lesson, Abraham is portrayed as a "friend of God." As you teach each lesson, make a list of questions regarding each person studied, then use those questions as review. Ask the students, "Who am I?" and give them "clues" about that person from your list. This activity can continue throughout all thirteen lessons and will give the students a good understanding of who each person is that you have studied.

Sword Drill

The Bible is our best defense against Satan, and we can use it as our "sword" to fight off sin by knowing what God's Word contains. This activity helps students remember where to locate books of the Bible.

Ask students to close their Bibles. You choose a book of the Bible, tell it to the students, and once you say, Go!", students may look up that book as fast as they can. Ask students to close their Bibles again, give them another book to look up, and say "Go!" You may keep a tally of points, if you wish, as a challenge for the students to see who finds the book the fastest. Once they are familiar with the books of the Bible,

Notes

you may ask them to look up individual verses referred to in the lessons. The first student who finds the verse, may read it. You may use this activity in subsequent lessons. Students will learn that when you announce "Sword Drill!," they are to close their Bibles and prepare to find what you choose to have them look up. If you have students who are consistently the first ones to find the verses, pair them up with a student who needs help in this area and work as teams, keeping points again to see which team finds it first.

Lesson I

The greatest hero of the Jewish people was Abraham. It is good to begin a series on the "Leaders in Israel" with Abraham. He was the founder of the nation of Israel, called of God for that purpose. All Jews, therefore, count their ancestry from him. Each of the leaders we will study in this series will have a place in the affections of the Jews, but none so much as Abraham.

The Aim

Abraham was called the friend of God for some very good reasons. These can be summed up in the intimacy which was characteristic of the relations between Abraham and God. Basically, that friendship can be connected with Abraham's faith (James 2:23). This is the point of emphasis you should carry through this lesson.

The Form

The story form is chosen for this lesson in order to arouse the interest of the student in a "real life" situation. The principles of friendship are sometimes abstract. The story attempts to identify the friendship of the two girls with the things that made Abraham the "friend of God." The story form will appear again in a later lesson.

Lesson Suggestions

The student should read Genesis 12:1-22:19 in preparation for the lesson. However, the references in Isaiah, 2 Chronicles, and James would serve for a quick Bible drill. They give you also an opportunity to explain the use of a concordance or computer Bible program. Bring a concordance or computer Bible program to class with you for a demonstration of its use. You may use effectively the word "friend."

A key sentence for teaching this lesson is seen in Betty's mother's statement about learning "why" Abraham was called the friend of God. The first suggestion is that he talked to God on many occasions. The references listed are all in Genesis, and are too numerous for a Bible drill. However, the reference Exodus 33:11 is quoted in full in the text. It is the key to this section.

The second reason for the friendship is the boldness with which Abraham "bargains" with God concerning the souls in the sinful cities of the plain. Read the reference in Genesis 18:1-33 in class, if time permits, and have the students to comment on their impressions of the passage. The reference in the New Testament that supports this point should also be studied in class.

The third reason that is assigned for the friendship of Abraham with God is his willingness to offer his son. Return to James 2:21-24 for further comment. There is an opportunity in this passage to show that New Testament faith must have its works of obedience to be made "perfect." Remember that your students are at the age of accountability, or approaching it. Don't miss any opportunity to inject the plan of salvation into your lessons. Subsequent lessons will suggest other points of this nature to emphasize.

Notes

Let's Talk About The Lesson

Only five questions are given with this lesson, because they are discussion questions.

1. In this question, your demonstration on the use of a concordance will be helpful. If you have time at the close of the lesson, let the students practice using the concordance or online Bible.
2. In this question, you should encourage discussion of any comparisons or contrasts in the friendships.
3. Here is an opportunity to review the three reasons for the friendship of Abraham and God found in the lesson.
4. This question is designed to reinforce the lesson of the importance of friendship. The answer is obviously, "yes."
5. Review the willingness of Abraham to offer his son as a sacrifice. Ask the students about their willingness to obey hard commands.

A Note on the Series

Each lesson in this quarter of study will be designed to be "practical." What we mean is that each lesson will have an application which will be reinforced by New Testament authority. In most cases, this important feature of the lessons will appear at the close of the lesson. These Old Testament stories are interesting to the junior-age student, and he may want to learn more of the "facts." You must be careful, therefore, not to be diverted from the aim of the lesson. Make sure that you leave yourself time to establish firmly the aim of each lesson.

Juniors are a fidgety group. Their interest span is somewhat longer than Primaries, but do not be tempted to challenge that span by dwelling too long on a certain point. Balance the lesson as well as you can between catering to the student, and concentration on the lesson goal.

Notes

Lesson 2
Moses – Deliverer of Israel

Next to Abraham, Moses holds the highest place in the mind of the Jews. He was the Lawgiver (actually, the law-receiver). At the time when the children of Israel were molded into a nation, Moses was the leader. He worked great miracles by the authority of God to deliver Israel out of Egyptian bondage. It is no wonder, then, that he was considered one of the greatest "Leaders in Israel."

The Aim

The aim of this lesson is to draw a contrast between the work of Moses as a deliverer, and that of Christ. The contrast is seen in the fact that Moses accomplished a physical deliverance from Egypt for the Israelites, while Jesus provides a spiritual deliverance from sin. This aim fits the general goal of this series to point out the New Testament principles in the Old Testament stories.

The Form

This lesson begins with a New Testament incident, because the defense of Stephen centers around the story of Moses. The first paragraphs of our lesson set the scene of the events leading up to the defense. Then, the story turns back to detail the events which brought the children of Israel into bondage in Egypt. The next paragraphs tell of the mistaken attempt of Moses to become a deliverer without the commission of God. His exile is mentioned, and the commission of God to return to Egypt after forty years. The deliverance of Israel is described in the following paragraphs. Finally, the comparison of Moses to Christ ends the lesson.

Lesson Suggestions

Since references in Acts 6 and 7 are scattered through the text of the lesson, it is hoped that the student will read these chapters in preparation. The students who are not familiar with the subject matter of the book of Acts should be told briefly that it is a history of the growth of the early church, and is useful in learning the plan of salvation.

The church had grown to the point that it was being considered a threat, and was inviting persecution. The actions of Stephen were typical of the boldness exhibited by the early Christians. They did not shrink from the consequences of their preaching. Stephen is to be commended for his willingness to "debate" with his opponents. The injustice of the enemies of Stephen can be seen in their bribing false witnesses, and their stubborn refusal to obey the truths of Stephen's defense.

In his defense, Stephen rehearses the events from Abraham to Moses in a methodical fashion, but his description of the work of Moses is more in detail. In Stephen's defense, and in our text here, we have prepared the ground for the introduction of Moses as a "deliverer" by speaking of the promise made by God to Abraham.

Moses grows up under very special and providential circumstances, but when he grows to manhood, he desires to be with his people. He sees their suffering, and even intervenes in one instance. The supposition that Stephen mentions in Acts 7:25 is a key to the lesson. Moses was hoping to be recognized as a deliverer, but he was rejected by the Israelites.

Show the students that forty years had to pass before God was ready to use Moses, but when God was ready, he put powerful tools in his hands. When he returns to Egypt, he is accepted by the people who have rejected him. This is the point which we have applied to Christ in the lesson. Stephen also applies the idea, showing that Moses spoke of a deliverer like himself, who would come by the direction of God.

It is important to emphasize the point that there is no salvation in any other but Christ. The importance of believing in and obeying Christ cannot be stressed too much. Christianity has much competition in our modern world. And, even within the confines of the religious world which attaches itself to Christ, modernists discredit Christ. You stand at an important phase in the development of young minds to show them the truth concerning Christ. He is divine; He is chosen of God; He alone has the power to save them from the consequences of sin.

Be sure to establish the difference in time between the events of Moses and the telling of those events by Stephen. You should recognize that your students have different levels of perception as to time. It is helpful to make a "time" chart and keep it posted on the wall of the class room. In each lesson, you can make reference to the position on the chart which relates to the Old Testament story. Many Bibles have a chart of this nature which you could copy and enlarge.

Questions

(The answers to the True-False questions are nearly all obvious, except the last two, # 7 and #8. The answer to both of these questions is "True," but they are given to afford the teacher an opportunity to illustrate how God has used angels to bring His messages to men. To speak to an angel was, consequently, the same as speaking to God.)

1. false
2. false
3. true
4. false
5. true
6. false
7. true
8. true

Notes

Notes

Lesson 3

Aaron – The First High Priest

The Aim

The aim of this lesson is to show the fulfilment of the office of high priest in the Old Testament by Aaron as the first, and Jesus as the last priest.

The Form

This lesson is in the form of a story from real life. Actually, the ceremony of the dedication of the priests is described in some detail. You will be able to arouse great interest, if you tell it in an animated way. Five points should be kept in mind when telling a story. (1) Use an attention grabber. (2) Make it interesting (use suspense, etc.). (3) Reveal the aim of the story. (4) Arouse curiosity about certain parts of the story. (5) Try to use a surprise ending or a unique twist to the application of it.

In this particular story-lesson, you might follow these suggestions:

- *Attention Grabber.* Bring some remnants of linen, purple, scarlet, and blue cloth; pass these around to the class for student comments on their beauty.
- *Make it interesting.* Try to develop the drama of the ceremony described by painting a word picture of the progressive steps of the event.
- *The aim of the story.* Since the object of this lesson is to compare Aaron's priesthood to that of Christ, ask the class to remember that the story deals with Christ's priesthood, too. This reminder will help develop the lesson.
- *Arouse curiosity.* Several points in the lesson adapt to this suggestion. Raise questions as to the significance of the breastplate, or the purpose of their washing.
- *Surprise twist.* The fact that Christ is the last High priest because He never dies provides a natural "twist" for ending the lesson.

Lesson Suggestions

1. A Ceremony of Dedication. You may have a desire to dwell too long on the preparations made by the Israelites for the building of the Tabernacle and the making of the Priest's garments. The reference given in the first paragraph (Exod. 35:4-29) is too long to read in class. This reference is provided for the benefit of the students' home study.

In the second paragraph, you may want to give a brief description of the arrangement of the Israelite camp (Num. 2) and the plan of the Tabernacle (Exod. 40).

In paragraph three, Moses and Aaron are mentioned by name, but Aaron's four sons are not. One of the assignments for the student is to find the names of these men. One reference for this is Leviticus 10:1, 12.

Notes

2. The Ceremony Begins. In the first paragraph of this section, reference is made to the washing of Aaron and his sons. A great laver, or bowl, of water was provided in the Tabernacle courtyard for this. The lesson suggests that privacy was maintained for this part of the ceremony, in view of the language which says that an exchange of old garments for the new was involved. Some commentators believe that this section of the courtyard was shielded from view by a screen across the gate of the courtyard. However, it is held by others that the Altar of Burnt Offerings could be seen by the worshippers, and it was just inside the gate of the Courtyard.

You may wish to connect the washing of Aaron and his sons with baptism in the New Testament. Use Romans 6:1-6 for this, or Hebrews 10:19-22. Also, use 1 Peter 2:9 to show that baptized persons are priests.

In paragraph two, the special dress of the high priest is described in detail. The linen breeches were given by God to protect the modesty of the priests. The breastplate was apparently made of cloth, with gold mountings for the precious stones. You may want to find some examples of these precious stones to show to the class. Some rock collector may have some examples of these that he would loan you for this purpose. One can find a picture of the garments worn by the High Priest on various internet sites. These stones are mentioned in Exodus 39:8-21. The use of the Urim and Thummim is mentioned in Numbers 27:18-21.

In paragraph three, a distinction is made between the high priest and the "regular" priests. Show the students, if time permits, the distinctions between the duties of the regular priests, and those of the high priest. Regular priests trimmed the lamps and replenished the incense in the tabernacle daily, they ate the shewbread and replenished the loaves once a week, and they handled the daily sacrifices. The High Priest was privileged to perform the atonement sacrifices once each year.

3. The Sacrifices. Much detail is given as to the manner of the sacrifices which has not been included in the lesson material. However, the scripture which tells of this is cited for the student, and he is encouraged to read this for himself.

4. The Priesthood is changed. In this section, you may want to impress upon the students that David, the king, was also a great prophet, and wrote many of the prophecies concerning Christ. He lived about a thousand years before Christ.

It may be well, in the use of Hebrews 7:11-12, to show that men shoudl respect the silence of the Scriptures. Moses "spoke nothing" concerning priests from the tribe of Judah, so Christ could not fulfil the prophecy of David, or serve as a priest while the Old law stood. Even so, we cannot change any specific law today by adding something in the area of silence. For example: we cannot add musical instruments to our worship, because the scripture specifies vocal singing.

5. Christ, the New High Priest. Several references are made in this section to the book of Hebrews, because a lengthy argument is made by the writer of this book on this subject. You would do well to read this complete argument, in order to be familiar with the way each of these references may apply to it.

Notes

The main emphasis in this section is to provide the solutions to the two problems raised in section four. The law was changed, or taken away, to accommodate the establishment of Christ as a High Priest. He is able to serve forever as high priest by virtue of an endless life.

The lesson ends on a note to exalt Christ as our compassionate and able High Priest to take away our sins. Remember always that this age group is impressionable with such things, and that they are also at the approximate age of spiritual responsibility. The words you can speak to move them to obey the gospel will be well received.

Questions

1. The obvious answer is yes, but show that many denominations have elaborate ceremonies, because of their adherence to Old Testament forms.

2. The exchange of the garments and the washing.

3. The gold and precious stones would run the cost of the garments into tens of thousands of dollars by today's standards. The student is asked only to guess on this question.

4. No.

5. The change of the law was required, and the new High Priest would somehow have to be a priest forever.

6. Christ solved the problems by changing the Law, and by rising from the dead to live forever.

7. Yes.

Search Your Bible

a. The answer here is in Leviticus 10:1, 12.

b. Genesis 14 has the story of Melchizedek.

Lesson 4

Joshua – The Captain of Israel

The age group you are teaching is subject to hero worship. Therefore, you are afforded an opportunity to emphasize this trait of heroism in Joshua.

The Aim

The story of Joshua, and his "step by step" development as a leader in Israel, should give you an excellent opportunity to teach your students the virtues of loyalty, courage, and trust in God. Apparently, Moses recognized these virtues in Joshua from the very beginning of their association. These virtues are not held in high esteem in our modern society, but impressionable minds can be directed toward them. Juniors are of that sort of material.

The Form

The narrative form of the lesson is divided into steps. Each one of these steps provides a form of progression to show the rewards of developing traits such as were possessed by Joshua. It should not have to be said that such traits are certainly characteristic of every faithful Christian.

To arouse the interest of the students and to stimulate their participation in the lesson, ask them at the completion of the discussion of each "step" to suggest the best word that would describe the character of Joshua at that point.

After Step # 1, you may hear suggestions such as: Bravery, Courage, Leadership (your choice of a word most fitting should then be written on the chalkboard).

After Step # 2, you may hear such suggestions as: Loyalty, Devotion, or Submission (again, your choice of these suggestions should be written down).

After Step #3, the students may suggest: Confidence, Courage, Trust, etc. (write down your choice).

After Step # 4, you may hear: Success, Leadership, etc.

This exercise will help to establish a train of thought, and will be excellent material for review at the end of the lesson.

Lesson Suggestions

The first section of the lesson (before discussion of Step # 1) is mostly introductory.

You may wish to define the word "pagan" in the first paragraph, since some of the students may not be familiar with that word. Define it simply as people who worshipped false gods.

The term "secret weapon" is used to provide a means to coordinate the various sections of the lesson.

Step #1: Some of the conclusions drawn by the author in this sec-

Notes

Notes

tion are based simply on reasoning, and not on biblical information. He presumes that Israel was without trained warriors and weapons. The author has attempted to label all such suppositions with terms such as "probably" and "we can imagine."

You should remind the students that miraculous help for Israel was very common to their journey. Water from a rock, manna from heaven, and clouds to lead were all a part of the pattern.

Step #2: We may presume that Joshua won the respect of Moses in the courageous way he went out to fight the Amalekites, since the next reference to him in the Bible shows him as a "minister" to Moses. Because he had become a man of war, he naturally interprets the noise of revelry as the noise of war.

It would be worthwhile to show that Joshua was fortunate to not be present when the children of Israel became corrupt in their behavior. Show the student that he does not have to be present where sins are being committed in order to learn the lesson of their sinfulness. Paul teaches that such an idea is wrong (Rom. 3:7-8; 6:1-2). Joshua was made stronger by merely being an observer. He saw the sin, saw the punishment and learned the lesson of complete submission to the will of God.

Step # 3: By the time that the Israelites are ready to send in spies to the land of Canaan, Joshua is recognized as a prince or a ruler of his tribe, Ephraim.

It is important to help the student realize that Joshua strongly urged the people to comply with the command of God, but he completely separated himself from the actual attempt made by the people, after God had predicted their failure. When you are on God's side, you do not compromise yourself with the schemes and well-meaning "works" of men who do not act under the authority of Christ.

Step #4: For the years of faithful service, Joshua is rewarded by God to be the successor of Moses. The detailed accounts of the conquest of Canaan show the complete dependence of Joshua upon God and His help. The real soldier and captain was the Lord, and Joshua gives Him credit in the reference given in the text, Joshua 24:2-15. This probably should be read aloud to the class.

The connection of Christ to Joshua is loose, but it attempts to show that Jesus followed the example of dependence upon God for His spiritual victories.

The Questions

Answers: 1. No, 2. No, 3. Yes, 4. No, 5. Yes, 6. No, 7. No, 8. Yes, 9. Yes, 10. Yes.

Discussion Question

Joshua was not present when they devised their sins or disassociated himself from their sinful acts. His reward was that he entered into Canaan, while the rebels died in the wilderness.

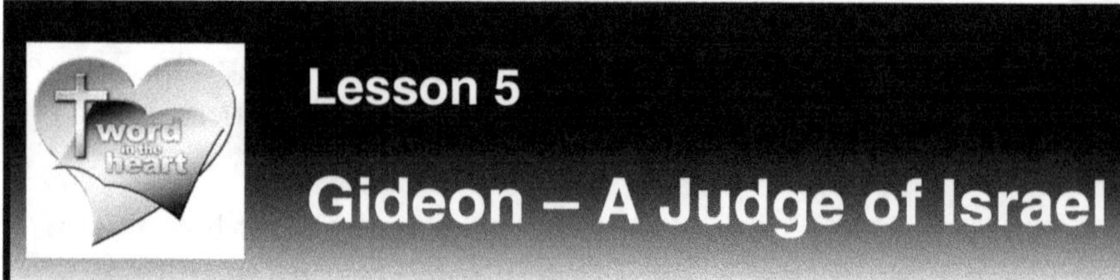

Lesson 5

Gideon – A Judge of Israel

Notes

Wide-eyed young readers of the Bible usually thrill to the stories of the Judges of Israel. Samson, Deborah, Jephthah, and Gideon stand among the favorites. The students should be encouraged to read the book of Judges from the Bible or from a reliable Bible story book.

The Aim

If the story of Gideon has any main theme, it is the power of God to take humble and brave men to accomplish tasks that seem overwhelming. The faith of the men and the power of God combine to conquer obstacles of great proportion.

The story of Gideon, however, has many lessons, and it is the desire of the author of this lesson book to give a broader view of the life of Gideon, so as to help the teacher choose the point of emphasis which he considers most appropriate to his students. Such points will be suggested by the lesson comments below.

The Form

The lesson material is divided into six sections, the first two of which form some background material important to the understanding of the lesson. The next three deal with the accomplishments and character of Gideon, and the last section compares the character of Gideon to the Lord Jesus Christ.

Lesson Suggestions

1. The Period of the Judges (Judg. 2:6-23). This background material is taken from an early chapter of Judges that tells of the conditions which prevailed in the time of the Judges of Israel. This section shows the importance of faithful leadership in keeping God's children faithful. Most people are simply followers, they do not lead. Among your own students, you have a majority of followers and only a few potential leaders. It is good to impress the importance of faithful leadership to both followers and leaders.

The children of Israel had ample opportunity to learn of the worship of Baal and other pagan gods. Some of the Canaanites who had occupied the promised land before the Israelites came had not been altogether destroyed or driven out. When God and His power became less important to the people, it was natural for them to adopt the idols of the Canaanites.

When the Israelites would defect from God, suffer from their defection, and call again on Him, God answered with saviors who had one thing in common, faith. The reference in Hebrews 11 mentions four judges and Barak, the captain who helped the woman judge, Deborah.

2. The Times of Gideon (Judg. 6:1-6). These verses paint a rather descriptive picture of the severity of the oppression of Israel. They record the oppression principally of the Midianites. You might want to research the histories of these peoples. The Midianites were descendants

Notes

of Abraham and his concubine, Keturah (Gen. 25:2ff). Moses found refuge with them while exiled from Egypt, and married the daughter of one of their priests (Exod. 2:15ff). They gradually grew more and more hostile to the Israelites after they left Egypt and moved to occupy the land of Promise. Gideon's war with them broke much of their power (Judg. 8:28). The Amalekites are mentioned in other lessons of this series (see lessons on Joshua and Samuel). The Ishmaelites are also identified with Abraham and Sarah's handmaiden, Hagar. They are often associated with the Midianites in the Bible, and are the ancestors, in part, of the modern Arabs.

3. Gideon is Chosen to Save Israel (Judg. 6:7-32). You will want to explain that conquering armies often find it much easier to control their conquered people when they destroy their food supplies. By this means, it is almost impossible for the conquered people to mount a strong resistance.

Gideon apparently followed the course of passive resistance by hiding his threshing operation, but he must have had a reputation as a "mighty man of valor," an heroic soldier. He could not see how Israel could overcome the harsh conditions imposed on them.

You could compare his reluctance to serve as the savior of Israel to that similar humble attitude in Moses (Exod. 4:1-17). His caution is evident when he chooses night (darkness) to cover his destruction of the altar of Baal. He is still discovered, but his bravery is defended by his father, and the men of his village take no further action.

The point is made in the lesson that idols have no power. This theme is found elsewhere in the Old Testament (read Hab. 2:18-21; Psa. 135:15-18).

4. God Gives Gideon the Victory (Judg. 6:33-8:13). Much of the detail of the story of the reduction of Gideon's army is left out in order to save space. Some attention, however, should be given to the reason for reducing an army that was already outnumbered heavily by the enemy.

The success of the device used by Gideon to scare the Midianites into killing one another can be compared to modern tricks of war which deceive the enemies. (Example: American bombers in World War II dumped basket loads of tinfoil over Germany to fool the enemy radar regarding their number and destination. Anti-aircraft guns were thus prevented from accurate shooting).

5. The Wisdom of a Great Judge. Two examples of the practical wisdom of Gideon are given to show the general character of men chosen by God as Judges.

The first instance of his wisdom shows his diplomacy in dealing with the Ephraimites. He degraded his own achievements to bolster the pride of the Ephraimites and placate their anger.

A ruler must have the power of discipline over his subjects and must be a man of his word. Gideon made threatening promises to the men of Succoth and Penuel to punish their refusal to aid his small army. When he returned victorious, he fulfilled these promises, and showed the price to be paid for refusing help to the Lord's cause.

6. Gideon and Christ. The comparisons made between the Judgeships of Gideon and Christ are inserted merely to inject New Testament teaching into the lesson. Their realms are contrasted so as to exalt the spiritual judgeship of Christ. In Christ we have great combinations of Judge, King, Master, Teacher, Savior, and Servant. To help the student to appreciate the character of Christ and to glorify Him is one of the main objects of all Bible Teaching.

Notes

Questions

Because it was necessary to be brief in the text of this lesson, the student has a good exercise to read and find the information asked for in the questions. Instead of providing the answers to the questions, we provide the teacher with the references where the answers are found.

1. Judges 6:15, 2. Judges 6:17-21, 3. Judges 6:32, 4. Judges 6:32, 5. Judges 7:2-3, 6. Judges 7:4-7, 7. Judges 7:16, 8. Judges 8:30.

Notes

Lesson 6

Samuel – Last Judge of Israel

Old Testament studies are valuable because of the practical application of the lessons. Paul said, of the events recorded in the Old Testament, ".. . these things happened unto them by way of example; and they were written for our admonition" (1 Cor. 10:11). Thus, the lesson draws a practical application from the experiences of Samuel, instead of adding to the historical information given in the lesson on Gideon. As the last judge of Israel, Samuel was a transitional figure between the period of the judges and the period of the kings.

The Aim

The character of Samuel makes a deep impression upon the pages of the Bible, and though he had many qualities, we emphasize his devotion. His duty to God and his love of man combines to cause him to become a willing instrument of correction and rebuke. It will be well to point out to the students that Samuel's efforts to correct those he love did not change their conduct, for neither Eli nor Saul escaped the consequences of their attitudes. In spite of the possibility of failure, however, and in spite of the difficulty of correcting those we love, we must still make the effort.

The Form

The lesson begins in a narrative form, and brings in some information about the "first-born" and their redemption with the Levites. In this portion, it will be well to set the scene for your students in a dramatic fashion. Then, the lesson moves to draw examples from the early and later life of Samuel. The admirable characteristic of Samuel is then reflected in the actions and statements of the Apostle Paul from the New Testament.

Lesson Suggestions

Again, we warn the teacher that conjecture on the part of the author is usually defined with qualifying terms such as "may" and "probably." Such is the case in the first paragraph. You should be thoroughly familiar with the lesson material, so that your own conjectures (which should be rare) can be as well defined.

Given to God

The terms used in reference to Samuel imply that he was a rather young child when he experienced his nocturnal visit from God. He had been brought to the tabernacle as soon as he weaned (in Bible times about the age of three, according to the *International Standard Bible Encyclopedia*).

The laws which authorized the dedication of the first-born males did not provide for exempting one from the provision for his redemption. However, Hannah had promised not to redeem him, and the Lord honored her vow. Under ordinary circumstances, a Levite would have taken Samuel's place in the service of the tabernacle.

Notes

Samuel Hears a Voice in the Night

Reference is made to 1 Samuel 3:1 to explain why Samuel did not recognize the voice in the night as the voice of God. There were few prophets, and few instances of prophecy during that period. This helped to establish Samuel's reputation as prophet quickly and broadly (1 Sam. 3:19-4:1).

Eli, the priest, had been too lenient with his sons. They had corrupted themselves, and had brought their vile practices right into the House of God. As a father, Eli had to bear the consequences of failing to restrain them. In this case, God had become so angry that he promised that their sins would not be "expiated by sacrifice, forever!" (Examples of this nature are rare in the Bible; another appears in 2 Chron. 36:15-17.) Such a terrible message was given to Eli, indirectly, through the voice of a child. There was a lesson in this method for the child. Though he was afraid to tell Eli, he was persuaded to fulfil his duty. It is significant that he "hid nothing" of the message, and you should tie this statement to Paul's in Acts 20:27.

To Tell The Truth or Not

This section merely poses the question of the lesson, or defines the problem facing the faithful Christian.

Samuel Does His Duty Out of Love

This section describes the second incident in which Samuel needed to rebuke a friend. One sentence of the section mentions the fact that the period of the Judges was ending with Samuel. You should relate this to the last lesson on Gideon, but do not dwell on the point. Also mentioned is the failure of Saul to destroy Amalek. If you have the temptation, as some teachers do, to be diverted from the thrust of the current lesson into other channels, you will fail to bring home the main aim of the lesson. Again, therefore, do not dwell overlong on this point.

The fact that Samuel mourned for Saul is indication that he loved him, and would have preferred to see Saul's attitude change for the better. Samuel's voluntary separation from Saul shows that he was willing to bear the consequences of his unheeded rebuke. Truth sometimes makes enemies, and at other times separates friends.

Paul, Another Example

Paul is shown to be consistent in his relationships. He clears himself of the "blood" of the Ephesians by speaking the whole truth. He tells the Galatians the truth about their defections, even though they may regard him as an enemy. And, finally, to the Corinthians, he has solace in the knowledge that his epistle of rebuke had made them "sorry after a godly sort." So, he treated all alike, because he loved all alike.

You will be best prepared to discuss this section with your students if you read the texts given with their contexts. The students may have some questions about the language used by Paul in these places, and the connections of the passages in 1 Corinthians with those of 2 Corinthians.

Notes

Lesson 7

David – King of Israel

We continue to follow the main idea behind the *Word in the Heart* series by making a practical application of the lesson, rather than presenting only its historical value. There are many traits to be found in the life of David which could be emphasized, but the trait of forgiveness seems to be the most highly developed one.

The Aim

We should desire to plant the principle of love for enemies into the minds of children at an early age. It is a difficult attitude to learn, after maturity has been reached. The impressionable Juniors will accept such a principle, when seen in its practical background. The contest between David and the brothers, Joab and Abishai, is a perfect setting for this demonstration.

The Form

First, some historical background information is given on David, his anointing by God, his service in the household of Saul, and his escape to exile. A skeleton history of the rest of David's life is given in the facts presented in the examples of David's attitude.

Second, several examples of the principle of forgiveness of enemies are cited.

Last, the attitudes of David are contrasted with those of the brothers, in the light of the teachings of Christ and the apostles.

Lesson Suggestions

As we have said before, the teacher must regulate the time he spends on details, so as not to obscure the main purpose of the lesson. The statements in the first two paragraphs of the lesson, and the historical details given elsewhere, could easily be expanded, but the teacher must resist the temptation. The third paragraph is important, in that it introduces the principle characters of Joab and Abishai. The scripture references given are inserted to confirm the statements preceding them, and to provide a source for the questions at the end of the lesson.

Examples

The five examples given should be read thoroughly in the Scripture by the teacher, before he presents the lesson. This will enable him to answer detailed questions of the students about the lessons. For economy of space, the stories are told in a very brief fashion, and many details are left out. The facts which remain are given to provide continuity for the examples. However, the teacher should concentrate on the aim of the lesson.

The Scripture references given at the close of examples # 2 and #4 are lengthy. The student should read these at home. Class time should not be used to read these aloud.

Notes

Since many names appear in the five examples, try to distinguish the names of Joab, Abishai, and David by emphasis, so that they will stand out from the secondary characters who are introduced. Your own familiarity with the characters will aid you to do this effectively.

David's Attitude vs. Joab's

In reading the story of David, one can sense the growing antagonism between David and Joab. Men who follow evil will grow worse and worse (2 Tim. 3:13), while men who follow after righteousness will grow better and better (2 Cor. 7:1). Therefore, the gap between the righteous and the wicked widens with every passing day.

Justice for the wicked

The fact that David would not undertake the punishment of Joab personally gives us the opportunity to show that, in New Testament times, we must not practice the law of vengeance. Rather, we should turn all such action over to God. We cannot judge our fellow men fairly, but we can trust God to be fair.

Questions: (answers)

1. Adullam (1 Sam. 22:1)
2. Jebusites (1 Chron. 11:6)
3. Bethlehem (1 Chron. 11:17)
4. A spear and a cruse of water (1 Sam. 26:11-12)
5. Hebron (2 Samuel 3:27)
6. Benjamin (2 Sam. 16:11)
7. Oak (2 Sam. 18:9,14)
8. Bichri (2 Sam. 20:6)

Discussion

The references given to the student in the lesson should be used by the teacher for study in this extra assignment.

Notes

Lesson 8

Elijah – A Religious Reformer

The importance of Elijah in the Bible cannot be ignored in view of his appearance with Christ on the Mount of Transfiguration. He represented the prophets. The Old Testament prophesied of his return, which Christ said was fulfilled by the coming of John the baptizer (Mal. 4:5-6; Matt. 11:11-14). Therefore, to include a lesson on the prophet Elijah is fitting in a lesson series on Leaders in Israel.

The Aim

The spectacular works of Elijah make an extremely dramatic presentation in themselves, yet the author has shown that Elijah acted very much alone in his reformation. Young people today have the increasing awareness that living the Christian Life is a lonely task. Even their friends from other religious groups seldom have the interest in spiritual things expected of a true Christian. Your students are at the age when they can make their spiritual choices, so they need to be encouraged to take a stand for Christ, even if they must stand alone.

The Form

The first section of the lesson is historical, tracing the series of events briefly which bring us to the time of Elijah. The teacher should be familiar with this transition material.

The next two sections describe the events of the drought and the contest on Mount Carmel.

The last section makes application, using the examples found in the previous two sections to demonstrate the loneliness of Elijah's stand against error.

Lesson Suggestions

1. From David to Ahab. There are many good lessons to be found in the history of the kingdom from the time of David to that of Ahab. Most of the comments in this section are important to a serious student, who wants to be knowledgeable in Bible history. The reason for the dividing of the kingdom, the dynasties of the kings of the divided kingdom, and the divergent spiritual courses each kingdom took are all important facts that could be briefly stressed by the teacher.

The Bible states that Ahab's sin was greater than Jeroboam's, and the teacher may wonder why this is so, since both errors involved idolatry. All the implications of Scripture suggest that the golden calves of Jeroboam were used to worship Jehovah in a perverted way. However, the worship of Baal turned people away from the worship of Jehovah altogether. Thus, Baal worship was more serious as an error than the worship of the calves.

Some practical explanation of the idea of reformation should be devised by the teacher, so that the students will understand the concept.

2. Elijah and the Famine. In the title of this section, the word famine

Notes

is used. It will be helpful to the understanding of the student for the teacher to picture for him the conditions which would result from the lack of rain for such a long period of time.

The quotation from James emphasizes the fact that Elijah's prayer was effective. It is used as an illustration of the power of prayer. Elijah's effectual prayer is also noted in the contest on Mount Carmel. This could be compared to the simple prayer of Jesus before the tomb of Lazarus (John 11:41-42).

The necessity for Elijah to hide from the wrath of King Ahab is the first illustration of the loneliness of the prophet. There were no others to aid him, apparently (though we hear of a hundred other prophets in 1 Kings 18:3), so the birds fed him and the wilderness hid him. When God dispatched Elijah to Zarephath, we find the second illustration of Elijah's lack of faithful company in Israel. Zarephath is in the region from which came Jezebel, the wife of Ahab. Elijah was in no great danger there, because that was probably the last place Ahab would have expected to find him.

The touching story of Elijah's stay with the widow is seen as an illustration of the providence of God toward the faithful. God did not give her a warehouse of meal or a tank of oil. He only supplied a daily ration which was used to feed an extra mouth.

3. The Contest on Mount Carmel. The object lesson given by Elijah to the people and to Ahab was very effective. Economy of space would not permit a more detailed description of this dramatic event, but you should encourage your students to read the whole text from the Bible, and you can add to this with emphatic statements of your own. It is evident that Ahab was impressed, since he was an eye witness to the event. But, Jezebel was only angry at the report of the destruction of her prophets and drove Elijah into hiding again.

4. Was Elijah Alone? You should mention that the despair of Elijah included asking God to take his life because he thought he was a failure (1 Kings 19:4). The passage we quote in the lesson, however, points to the loneliness of Elijah, and God's answer.

Consistent with the author's policy to connect each lesson with a New Testament principle, he compares the apostle Paul's lonely defense in Rome. Your students have not had the experience of feeling lonely in their effort to live for God, perhaps, but this lesson will condition them for this experience when it does come.

Questions

1. false
2. true
3. true
4. false
5. true
6. false
7. false
8. true
9. false
10. true

Notes

Lesson 9

Isaiah – Statesman and Prophet

Isaiah's unique contribution to the literature of the Old Testament cannot be appreciated by one who has not read it thoroughly, or who has not studied it in the light of the later history of the kingdoms of Israel and Judah. In this lesson, however, we take only one incident to show the place Isaiah filled as a statesman/prophet.

The Aim

We want the student to be impressed with the principle that only through obedience to the will of God without amendment or deviation can we hope for the promises connected with that obedience. Hezekiah's dependence on Isaiah's word gained deliverance from the Assyrians. The alien sinner's dependence on the plan of salvation will gain the remission of sins. This point is emphasized so many times in Scripture that it bears repeating many times.

The Form

The introductory section of the lesson sets the scene of the historical event described in it. The next section presents the background of the event, showing the mistake of Ahaz, and subsequent events which led up to the appearance of Rabshekah at the wall. The next section returns to the historical account of our story, and carries it through the appeal of Hezekiah to Isaiah. The next two sections discuss the importance of the prophet's work and his style of prophecy. The last section makes application from a New Testament example.

Lesson Suggestions

This lesson has dramatic possibilities, and the teacher can make the story live by animated reading of the lesson and the additions of pertinent detail. The wall of the city of Jerusalem was fortified against attack. Jerusalem was not impregnable, but it was a difficult city to besiege, since it had its source of water enclosed in the wall and was situated on a hill. However, the might of the Assyrian army was probably very impressive to the Jewish soldiers.

It may be necessary to explain the idea of rebellion to the students. A comparable example would be the revolution of the thirteen colonies against British rule in 1776.

The Mistake of Hezekiah's Father

Draw the distinction again in this lesson of the difference between the Kingdom of Judah and the Kingdom of Israel. This history is related in the first part of Lesson # 8. The submission of Ahaz to Assyria illustrates that he did not have any confidence in the help of God. This made it more difficult for Hezekiah to break away from Assyrian domination. The lesson notes, in passing, that Hezekiah tried to buy his independence through a gift of money. This probably was not the same thing that Ahaz was doing. Probably Ahaz was sending tribute to Assyria on a regular basis. Hezekiah hoped that one large gift would suffice to buy off Sennacherib. It did not work.

Since Isaiah said some things about the fault of trusting in the help of Egypt (Isa. 31:1-9), we may presume that the advisors of Hezekiah were seeking help from Egypt, though this is not stated specifically in the scripture.

Notes

The Assyrians Boast of Their Power

The Assyrians had been successful against several small nations in its vicinity, and at the time of Sennacherib's invasion of Judah, it was at its strongest. However, the Bible account records the defeat of Sennacherib before Jerusalem, and his return to Assyria. Archaeologists have uncovered many records of Sennacherib's campaign in Judah, and these confirm the Bible story in nearly every detail, except the defeat. It is reasonable to assume that a proud king, such as Sennacherib would not record this defeat in his annals.

The little dramatic account of the appeal of Hezekiah's advisors for Rabshekah to speak in a language unfamiliar to the soldiers on the wall can be embellished with detail by the teacher with good effect. Rabshekah was so confident of his power that he spoke directly to the men on the wall, and exposed his whole intent to them.

A Prophet of God Advises Kings

The section of Scripture referred to in this portion of the lesson is called the "burden" section of Isaiah (Isa. 13:1-24:23). The word "burden" is used to describe the weight of the message given through the prophet. All of God's promises are fulfilled, and Isaiah's prophecies concerning the destinies of nations are no less important than the prophecies concerning Christ.

Isaiah's writings contain many hopeful promises, as the lesson suggests, and his prophecies concerning the coming of Christ were designed to give hope to the Jews, even though they faced captivity. They would not be the ones to see the Christ, but they could realize that their descendants would have that privilege.

The Help of God is the Only Way

Since some of your students will have reached the age of responsibility in spiritual things, it is well to return now and then in applications of lessons to the theme of salvation. Christ's comments on the attempt of men to be saved by their own devices is appropriate in this place. It helps you to emphasize the need to obey only the will of God. When men trust in themselves or in man's ideas for salvation, they must be disappointed (Matt. 7:21 ff).

Expand the appeal of this lesson at the close with a brief account of the commands to be obeyed for the remission of sins.

Questions

1. He sought the help of Assyria rather than of God.
2. Egypt.
3. No.
4. No. They rent their clothes.
5. To Isaiah and to God.
6. God spoke through him concerning the destinies of nations.
7. No.
8. 185,000.
9. Hard.

Notes

10. No.

(NOTE: The students should use their own words to answer these questions.)

Notes

Lesson 10

Jeremiah – The Prophet Who Saw Jerusalem Destroyed

The work of Jeremiah must have seemed very frustrating to him, because he preached the destruction of Judah and Jerusalem in the knowledge that nothing the people could do would save them from it. In order for this lesson to be reasonable to your students, you must first impress them with the long history of disobedience that the people of God persisted in pursuing.

The Aim

We would impress the student, also, with the fact that he may not persist in disobedience to God without expecting some dangerous consequences. Students of this age group are very impressionable, and it is good to make sure that they understand the urgency of obedience to the gospel.

The Form

The first section of the lesson and the second division trace the history of the Kingdom of Judah from the death of good King Hezekiah to the last King, Zedekiah. The next section is long, and shows the place of Jeremiah in that history. He is shown in three interviews counselling the people of Jerusalem to surrender. The last section makes application of the story to the need of the student.

Lesson Suggestions

In the first two paragraphs of the lesson, the student is introduced to the character of King Manasseh, whose evil actions brought down the unswerving wrath of God upon Judah. It would be well for you to read the accounts of Manasseh in both 2 Kings and 2 Chronicles, in order to be able to add detail to the information about him in the lesson text.

In the second paragraph quotation from 2 Kings 21, you will probably need to define the meanings of some words and terms. The reference to the "Amorites" needs explanation. The term, "Amorites," generally describes the people who had formerly lived in the land of Canaan before the occupation of the Children of Israel. The phrase "remnant of mine inheritance" can be defined as "the survivors of the children of Israel."

God Does Not Change His Mind

You should review how God had formerly blessed the Jews when they had good kings, and when they turned away from idols. Now, however, even the reign of a good king will not cause God to repent of the destruction He promised. The rulers of Judah are shown to be unstable (because of their short time in ruling), and progressively deaf to the words of God through the prophets.

Jeremiah Prophesies Doom

In the first paragraph of this section, emphasize the fact that there was a terrible combination in false prophets on the one hand, and willing listeners on the other. All of the prophets of God pronounced the

Notes

doom of Judah, yet the people and the king thought they could escape this doom, and fought on to save themselves.

In every case, Jeremiah does not cease to tell of the impending fall of the nation, and his enemies grow increasingly angry at him. He escapes death only by the help of God. The theme of the whole lesson is summed up in the quotation from 2 Chronicles 36:16, "There was no remedy." The sad story of the fall of God's people is a strong example for us.

Jeremiah on the Side of God

Jeremiah is shown to be faithful to the Word of God, even though he appears as a traitor to the people. The last paragraphs show that we must also be careful not to impose upon the patience of God. The similarity between the words of 1 Thessalonians 5:3 and our story is unmistakable. Here is another chance for you to follow the appeal of the last lesson for the salvation of your responsible students.

Questions

1. Manasseh
2. Josiah
3. Jehoiakim
4. false prophets
5. Babylon
6. doom
7. traitor
8. surrender to the enemies
9. run out
10. longsuffering

Notes

Lesson 11
Esther – The Queen Who Saved Her People

The story of Esther is one of the highly dramatic moments in Bible history. Esther's courage is shown in the way she dared to risk her life for others. In preparation for this lesson, your students should have read the whole book of Esther. You should question them on this point, and insist that they read all references given in the lesson material.

The Aim

Again, our general aim is to find practical value in the lesson from the Old Testament, and to reinforce it from the New Testament. The emphasis is upon the courage of Esther, but more to the point, on her motivation for risking her life. This point is shown in the statements of Jesus and Paul at the end of the lesson.

The Form

We have returned to the story form in this lesson, in order to balance the use of this form in the earlier part of the book. We use the same character, Betty, in order to identify her with the students of her age in your class. There is also the interplay of Betty's father and mother which brings out the side lesson regarding the honoring of men by women. Make the story live for the students. The story is not of a spectacular event, but rather a common one. A family is spending a quiet evening at home. Use this setting to an advantage by asking the students if they ever spend time in such reading and discussion of Bible lessons with their parents. Encourage the practice.

Lesson Suggestions

The Bible discussion of Betty with her parents is started with a question about the gender of Bible heroes. They are nearly always men, but several women are mentioned in heroic situations in the Bible. You may wish to read from Hebrews 11:35 the mention of women in the account of great deeds there.

Mother's remark about reading a whole book of the Bible at a sitting is an opportunity for you to encourage better reading habits in your students.

For the benefit of the girls in your class, you may want to define the choosing of a new queen as a kind of "beauty contest." The difference here is that the women chosen by the king became his concubines. Save yourself some diverting questions by avoiding a full description of this section. When the children are in an older age group, they will be able to comprehend Old Testament marriage practices better.

Betty's questions about the meanness of the king helps to introduce the side discussion of the Bible teaching about the place of women in God's scheme. Do not spend too much time on this, but see that the students know the principles.

Betty's question about the "fast" is explained to a degree in the story. However, if the students want a fuller explanation, be prepared to give

Notes

them some information. Describe a "fast" as a period of abstinence from food or other things. The term "breakfast" simply means to "break a fast" by eating, after a night of abstention.

The implication of the story of Esther is that God preserved the Jews from destruction by His providential care. However, it is worthy of note that the name of God is entirely missing from the book of Esther. Since God has preserved the book for our learning, we must conclude that He had a part in the events that transpired.

Search Your Bible (answers)

1. 180 days
2. 7 days
3. Abihail
4. Bigthan and Teresh
5. A banquet of wine
6. Haman
7. Hanging
8. Second to the King
9. By obeying His commands.
10. Those who do "evil works."

Lesson 12
Ezra – Reformer After the Captivity

Notes

We have stressed before, and here again, the importance of developing religious heroes for children of this age group. The story of Ezra has no great physical deed to attract the attention and admiration of the children. He is, in a simple way, only a Bible teacher. He had "prepared his heart to seek the law of the Lord, and to do it." This preparation was vital to his success as a Bible teacher, and it will be just as vital for you. Heroic deeds do not merely consist of fighting battles or performing great miracles. They also serve who only stand and teach.

The Aim

Ezra's story is useful in showing the students that they have a good example in the attitude of the people toward their teacher and toward his instruction. The students should be encouraged to follow the example of the Jews in correcting sins before punishment is due. To learn by example is important to the Christian.

The Form

The first part of the lesson graphically describes the scene of the Jews gathered in the great rain to do the will of God. We use a form of "flash-back" technique to recount the details of history leading up to the scene depicted. This lesson connects historically to lesson 10, rather than to lesson 11. The dating of the events of Esther falls after the return of the Jews to Judah and Jerusalem.

After historical background is given, Ezra is introduced. His discovery of the great moral problem among the Jews and the solution of that problem are found in the next section. The event of his great "Bible Class" is treated under a separate heading, because it appears in the book of Nehemiah. As is customary with the author, the last section is used for the application of the lesson.

Lesson Suggestions

Try to assist the imagination of the student in the first part of the lesson to see the great scene described. Your own imagination should be fruitful in this. Ask the students if they ever have attended a great event in the rain.

The Jews Return From Captivity

This lesson connects historically with lesson 10 about Jeremiah the prophet. You will be better equipped to teach this lesson, if you review that lesson before class time, and remind your students of some of the events of lesson 10 during class. Use a Bible map to show the positions of the various countries mentioned in this part.

Note that several references are given in this section from several books of the Bible. Some of the references are from the prophets and some from the historical books. You may wish to test the students' ability to find these references, but don't spend too much time in this.

Notes

Ezra Has a Plan

In this section, you should emphasize the importance of Ezra's determination to establish a foundation of truth for the people of God. It was not enough for them merely to rebuild the temple. They needed to be made spiritually strong through Bible study. You may want to tell the students more in detail about the work of the Scribes. Use a Bible dictionary to inform yourself about their work.

The interest that Artaxerxes had in providing for offerings for himself and his family shows that the knowledge of God was widespread, even among pagan people.

Ezra Finds a Problem

Ezra probably hoped to find that some progress had been made in Jerusalem regarding spiritual growth. Instead, he found that the people were falling into the sin that had caused much of their downfall before. They were marrying women of the pagan tribes of Canaan and were liable to the idolatrous influence of these women. Ezra was deeply disturbed by this.

Ezra expressed his concern in the "public" prayer before the temple. The people heard, and were sorry for their obvious sin. They realized that they could not repeat the sins of their fathers without suffering the same consequences. God is consistent. "Every sin and transgression receives a just recompense of reward" (Heb. 2:2).

The solution to the problem had to be just as drastic as the problem itself. Show your students that the Law of God had been violated and the only way it could be undone was to undo those acts of disobedience. Many people today will often fail to obey the truth, because it inconveniences them. They do not love the truth more than they love themselves. This point should be emphasized to the young minds in your charge, so that the proper foundation can be laid. Help them to love the truth more than anything or anyone else.

Ezra's Great Bible Class

Part of the solution was to teach the Jews the Law so that they would not make so many mistakes in the future. The Bible class is vital to establishing a foundation of obedience in young minds.

We Learn From Other's Examples

The examples given in this section are illustrations of what has happened to others, when they did not obey the Will of God. The warnings are calls to remember these consequences and to avoid them. This lesson can be used to show the value of repentance as a part of one's salvation.

Use Your Dictionary

This form of question has not appeared before in this lesson book. It will, however, give your students some practice in using an English dictionary. It is difficult to write challenging material in conservative space without using some words that may not be in the vocabulary of Juniors. Some of these words are from the Bible, but some are not. You should try to build the biblical vocabularies of your students at all times.

Lesson 13

Nehemiah – Rebuilder of the Walls

Notes

The last lesson in this quarter concerns the record of a man who had a consistent, almost stubborn, devotion to duty. Nehemiah showed qualities of moral leadership outside of the realm of the priesthood and the prophets. He was "secular" in his activities, but the Bible has recorded his story with the same sort of commendation applied to spiritual leaders.

The Aim

The Christian must have a sense of devotion to duty which cannot be distracted. Those who would do good will have opposition, sometimes moral, sometimes physical. The work which we do for Christ must be too important to allow any enemy of truth to hinder it.

The Form

The subject material of this lesson divides itself naturally into subtitles. The first three paragraphs deal with the events which led up to the return of Nehemiah to Jerusalem. The next section shows the general response of the enemies of the Jews. Then, their four methods are considered in order. The final section, as usual, is the New Testament application of the lesson.

Lesson Suggestions

The introductory material shows the number of men who rose to high places in the lands of the Captivity. This helps to introduce Nehemiah to the student. Even though a paragraph intervenes to tell of the conditions in Jerusalem before the lesson returns to consider Nehemiah, you should maintain the continuity of the introduction to him. His position as a cup-bearer can be discussed briefly to show that it was an important office.

Your students have already been told of the unapproachable position of the Persian kings in the lesson on Esther. For Nehemiah to be in the position of cupbearer to the king meant that he had gained the favor and confidence of a very important and powerful person. He could come close to the king at all times, and could converse with the king on an almost familiar basis. The friendship of the king was valuable, also. He gave material for the work which Nehemiah had planned.

Nehemiah's Return Disturbs the Enemy

The nation of Persia was a great conglomerate of smaller kingdoms and provinces. At this time, the government of the land of Canaan was probably loosely controlled by petty governors. It is possible that Sanballat and Tobiah were among this class. Even if they were not, they had attained positions of leadership among the non-Jewish population of the land.

Take some time to explain the necessity of having a fortified wall around the cities of that time. Most nations did not have rural police forces, and the main protection of the people was behind the walls of

Notes

fortified cities. The use of the wall to control the activity of the cities is seen in Nehemiah 13:15-22. This incident may help to build the image of the use of the wall in the mind of the student.

1st Method: Laughter

This is the first of the four sections dealing with the attempts of Saballat and Tobiah to prevent the building of the wall. The non-violent methods which were used first were very political, since even Sanballat and Tobiah probably feared the king of Persia too much to do otherwise. They did not resort to violent methods, until it appeared that the wall was about to be finished.

2nd Method: Discouragement

There is probably no greater hindrance to good works than the negative criticism of those who do not want to do them. Much of the work of the church requires persistence and a degree of patience. Because of this, it is easy to be discouraged by critics. The method used by Nehemiah here is a good one—to ignore the criticism and to continue the work with all the vigor possible. It is your task as a teacher to contribute to the conversion of the souls of your students, but it is also necessary to instill in them a desire to work for the good pleasure of God. Prepare their hearts for the attacks that may be made against their effort.

3rd Method: Violence

We do not have many enemies of truth today who will resort to actual violence, but they will actively oppose the work of others. If we show that we are willing to defend ourselves actively, meeting argument with better argument, we can sometimes avoid the opposition just as Nehemiah did.

4th Method: Compromise

Compromise is usually offered when all other things have failed. Make sure the students comprehend the meaning of compromise. When compromise is offered, we should carefully analyze the reasons for the offer, as Nehemiah did. We can then see that every offer to compromise is a partial surrender on the part of our opponent, and with a little more effort we can gain complete victory.

Working for Christ

Use the Bible references in this section for a Bible drill. There may be other verses on the same subject that you will want to add to these.

Reviewing the Lesson (Answers)

1. Yes
2. Cupbearer
3. The Temple
4. Artaxerxes
5. Night
6. Laughter, Discouragement, Violence, Compromise
7. Sanballat and Tobiah (others are mentioned)
8. No
9. Each carried weapons as well as tools
10. No.

Introduction to Teacher's Manual

The scope of the book of Genesis is vast, and a detailed study of it would take much longer than one quarter. Therefore, for this study, an effort has been made to choose the outstanding events and characters of the book. Likewise, effort has been made to present the lessons with a continuity that will help the students toward a better understanding of the historical development of the story of mankind. This is important, and you, as a teacher, should never let your students lose sight of the narrative which the book presents. A third aim of the lessons is to draw from these stories of ancient times applications which are meaningful to the lives of the children whom you teach. Good Bible teaching involves not only imparting facts but also inspiring students to do God's will as they learn to relate the principles to their own lives.

The format of the lessons in this book is uniform, conforming to the following outline:

- Memory Verse
- Some Facts to Learn
- Some Lessons to Apply to Your Life
- Questions

The scripture references for the lessons are listed. Students should be strongly encouraged to read these references. Because of the length of the book of Genesis, some of the texts are necessarily long; but much of the material is relatively easy-to-read narrative. The references have been chosen to present the high points of the lesson in as concise a manner as possible.

Students should be asked to memorize the verse selected for each lesson. These verses have been selected to impress the students further with the important point of the lesson and for beauty of language.

"Some Facts to Learn" presents the lesson story in simple, straightforward and concise narrative style. This is designed to help accomplish the aim of emphasizing the historical continuity of the lessons. Applications and illustrations of the principles of the story are reserved for another section of the lesson. It is hoped that the simple narrative style of this portion will combine with the reading of the scripture reference to make the students' understanding of the facts of the story as clear as possible.

In keeping with the title of this series, *Word in the Heart*, the section "Some Lessons to Apply to Your Life" is used to present applications and principles from the story that the children can relate to their own lives. Though your students may have learned the facts of these stories from early childhood, they may never have learned to apply the lessons to themselves. This effort is truly significant in a study of this kind, and needs to have much attention as you present the lesson. Children of this age have a great capacity for seeing the practical implications of

Notes

these stories, if you guide them carefully.

Questions are the exercises to be done with each lesson, and students should be urged to complete them before coming to class. It is a poor usage of class time to complete exercises that should have been done before coming to class. This will remove the incentive for study outside of class and can discourage even your best students. The exercises are purposely short to keep students from becoming discouraged by exercises that are too long and difficult to complete. Twenty-one different types of exercises have been used, and no one type is used more than twice in this book. Hopefully this variety will help keep the student interested in completing each lesson. The questions have also been arranged so that no exercise can be completely answered from the facts in the lesson narrative. Students must refer to the scripture text for some of the answers in each exercise. This is designed as encouragement to the students to read the text.

Your thorough preparation to teach each lesson is most urgent. So little time is available to teach so much, and good usage of your time is essential. Good preparation greatly aids your effective use of class time. To be prepared properly you must study the facts of each lesson until you know them thoroughly. Read and reread the Bible text, then use all other related materials to which you have access. Know each of your students—his background, personality, problems, ability, and interests. Present the lesson enthusiastically in clear language on the proper level for your students' understanding, trying always to relate the lesson to them personally.

Each lesson is preceded by a memory verse. Below you will find all of the memory verses for the 13 lessons which will be taught in this series of lessons. Please make these verses visible in the classroom and review frequently so that the students will apply them to their lives and memorize them.

- Lesson 1: "In the beginning, God created the heaven and the earth" (Gen. 1:1).
- Lesson 2: "So God created man in His own image; in the image of God He created him; male and female He created them" (Gen. 1:27).
- Lesson 3: "And the Lord God said, 'It is not good that man should be alone; I will make him a helper comparable to him'" (Gen. 2:18).
- Lesson 4: ". . . but of the tree of the knowledge of good and evil you shall not eat, for in the day that you eat of it you shall surely die" (Gen 2:17).
- Lesson 5: "Then the Lord said to Cain, 'Where is Abel your brother?' He said, 'I do not know. Am I my brother's keeper?'" (Gen. 4:9).
- Lesson 6: "But Noah found grace in the eyes of the Lord" (Gen 6:8).
- Lesson 7: "God said to Noah, "This is the sign of the covenant which I have established between Me and all flesh that is on the earth" (Gen. 9:17).
- Lesson 8: And God said to Abraham: "As for you, you shall keep My covenant, you and your descendants after you throughout their generations" (Gen. 17:9).
- Lesson 9: "And I will make My covenant between Me and you, and will multiply you exceedingly" (Gen. 17:2).

- Lesson 10: —"Then Isaac brought her into his mother Sarah's tent; and he took Rebekah and she became his wife, and he loved her. So Isaac was comforted after his mother's death" (Gen. 24:67).
- Lesson 11: "Do not be deceived, God is not mocked; for whatever a man sows, that he will also reap" (Gal. 6:7).
- Lesson 12: "But I say to you, love your enemies, bless those who curse you, do good to those who hate you, and pray for those who spitefully use you and persecute you . . ." (Matt. 5:44).
- Lesson 13: "And those who know Your name will put their trust in You; For You, Lord, have not forsaken those who seek You" (Psa. 9:10).

BULLETIN BOARD IDEAS: Since this series of lessons deals with the book of Genesis, a bulletin board could be developed with scenes depicting the days of creation, then add the Bible characters discussed in each lesson (Adam and Eve, Abraham, Sarah, Isaac, Jacob and Esau, Joseph). You could also develop a timeline, giving the students an idea of when each event took place, beginning with the Creation and ending with the last lesson of Joseph's family being reunited in Egypt.

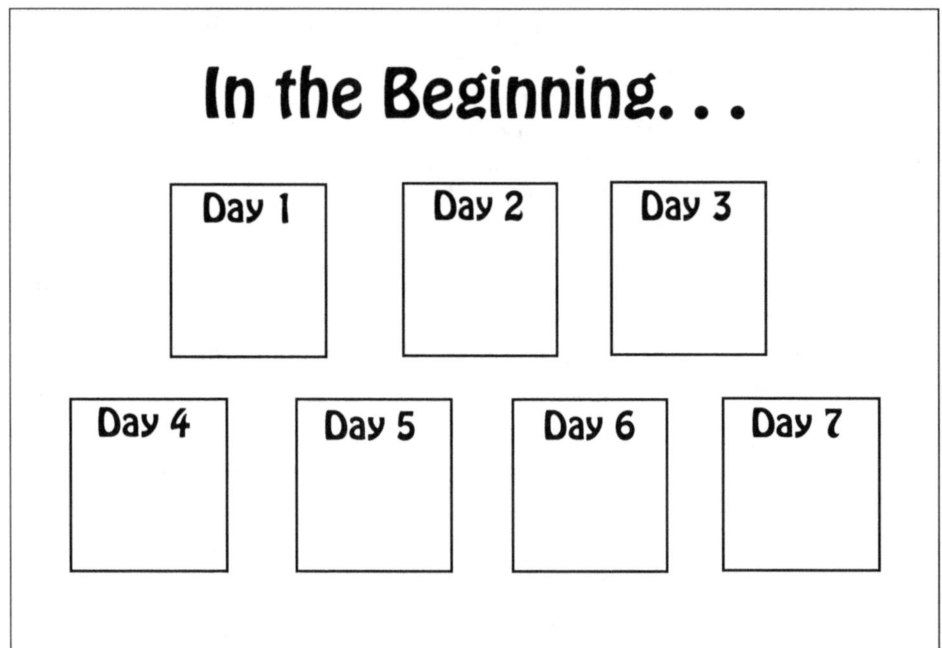

SUPPLEMENTAL ACTIVITIES: The lessons in this series are designed to show students God's purpose in the order in which He created things; God had a specific order in mind when He created each day and within each day, there was a purpose for the things He created on that particular day. It would be helpful for students to visualize the order of Creation, so that they may see His purpose.

Notes

Notes

The Creative Bible Teacher Always Obeys The Seven Laws of Teaching

1. The teacher must know that which he would teach.
2. The teacher must help the student to attend with interest to the lesson being taught.
3. The teacher must teach in a language understood by the student.
4. The teacher must begin with the known and proceed to the unknown.
5. The teacher must excite and guide the self-activities of the student.
6. The teacher must aim at getting the student to reproduce the *Word In The Heart*.
7. The teacher must complete, test, and confirm his work by review and application.

These laws are explained in detail in *The Seven Laws of Teaching*, by Milton Gregory.

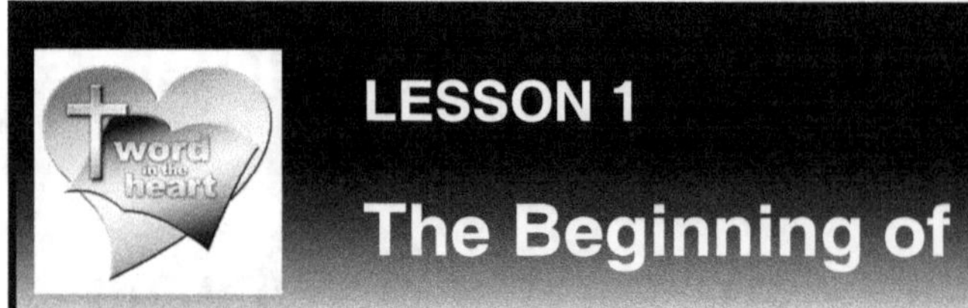

LESSON 1

The Beginning of the World

Notes

One of the first things that the smallest child in Bible school learns is that God made the heavens and the earth. The teacher impresses this fact on his young mind by a picture to color or a display on the flannel-board. A book of nature pictures soon impresses him that the things God made in the beginning are the things with which he is familiar in the world that he sees around him. It seems to be a simple thing for him to learn. Yet, as he grows, the scope of the story broadens and its import deepens. Indeed, as adults, we wrestle with the profoundness of the story of creation. The facts that seemed so simple to the small child become the object of intense and diligent study. The Genesis account of creation is one of the primary targets of the atheist, the infidel, and the modernist. It has been disbelieved, disregarded, and ridiculed. The mature Christian has been called upon to search more and more deeply into the account for the evidences that support his faith in God as the creator of the universe. Gone are the days when the atheistic science professor in the university is the first to challenge the young Christian's faith in the things he believes concerning the creation of the world. Today, the process begins much earlier in our system of education. Indeed, in many areas, the elementary school text books are full of atheistic and evolutionary teachings, presenting these ideas in such an insidious manner that even the child with a strong Bible background is apt to be caught unaware. The rapidly expanding, inquisitive minds of the juniors whom you teach are ripe for this kind of faith-destroying teaching. As teachers of this age group, we can no longer stick our heads in the sand and pretend that this threat does not exist and that we do not need to be prepared to deal with it.

The extent to which this area of thought should be discussed will, of necessity, vary in different localities, depending to what degree the children are exposed to atheistic and modernistic teaching in the schools. The child who has not had this teaching emphasized to him needs only to be warned that he will someday meet these ideas and those who will tell him that the Genesis account is not true. This child needs only the suggestion that this is to be expected, but it is not alarming. Then, when he does meet the situation, he will remember that his Bible school teacher knew about this and told him it would happen. He will feel a security in having been told about it beforehand. The child who has already been exposed has questions in his mind and needs answers to satisfy him and to strengthen his belief in what he has learned about God and the Bible. You, as a teacher, will need to determine to what extent you should pursue this discussion. Checking the text books used in the school system in your area will help you determine this. Some conversations with the parents of your students can give you helpful information. The preacher and the elders with whom you work may be able to help also.

The lesson text as presented endeavors to deal with the subject in

Notes

a matter-of-fact, positive manner in order to avoid upsetting a child who has not become aware of teachings that conflict with what he has learned about the Bible. At the same time it contains a warning that he will come in contact with those who do not want him to believe that God is the creator. The applications endeavor to lay some basic groundwork in suggesting areas of evidences on which he can build and strengthen the faith that will carry him through trials which will face him later in life. The ultimate saving of his faith in God and the Bible can well rest upon evidences he finds and not necessarily on his ability to answer every argument and quibble that an atheist can make.

The lesson material suggests some simple concepts of evidences which should be meaningful to the juniors. First, the idea of the reasonableness of the world having God as its maker is presented. Some examples of everyday things that require a maker are given with the application that anything as vastly complicated as our universe could not be an accidental happening. You will no doubt want to add other things to the list of examples. The wisdom of God as seen in the order of creation is discussed with examples designed to be meaningful to the children. Again your own examples and amplification will be of great benefit here.

Second, the Bible as the book of God's truth is discussed. The historical and scientific accuracy of the Bible statements pertaining to these areas is mentioned briefly. As time permits you may want to include some examples of this. Prophecy is also introduced. This may be a new area for many in your class and a more detailed definition and illustration will probably be required for their understanding. You will find children of this age fascinated with a discussion of God's prophecy.

Another area of study should be mentioned here for your consideration. Recent archeological findings have occasioned much study concerning the antiquity of man and the dating of early biblical events. The generally accepted chronology prepared by James Ussher in the seventeenth century which places the date of creation at 4004 B. C. is questionable. Other Bible chronologists suggest that the date of creation is from 6000 to 10,000 B. C. Though this is not a point which could be dealt with in detail in a class of children this age, you as a teacher will perhaps want to give it some additional study. *The Theme of the Bible* by Ferrell Jenkins and the *Wycliffe Historical Geography of Bible Lands* by Pfeiffer and Vos give some information along this line and they, in turn, refer to other works on the subject.

The first statement in God's revelation to man declares, "In the beginning God created the heavens and the earth." This is indicative of the significance of this lesson. It is one of the most important lessons you will ever teach.

Bring in magazines which contain many pictures of nature to be used for this activity. Create a collage of the Days of Creation, by taking an 8 ½ x 11 piece of paper, construction paper, or poster board and write "DAY 1" at the top. Have students find examples of light, day and night, or darkness to glue onto the collage. Continue this activity for "DAY 2" by looking for pictures of sky and water (Gen 1:6-8). Make additional collages for Creation Days 3-7. This activity may take more than one class period to finish.

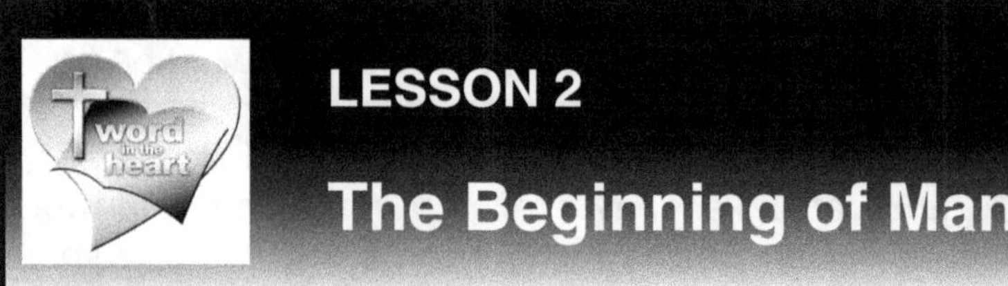

LESSON 2

The Beginning of Man

Notes

The Genesis account of God's creation of man has been attacked by the same disbelief that has attempted to destroy faith in God as the creator of the world and in the Bible as the inspired word of God. The evolutionist joins the atheist, the infidel, and the modernist in their efforts to discredit the inspired record of the beginning of the world and of man. Just as the very small child has learned that God made the heavens and the earth, so has he also learned that God made Adam and Eve and placed them in the Garden of Eden. But, in all probability, before he completes elementary school, both his text books and some of his teachers will have told him that man was not created in the beginning in God's image as we know him today, but rather that he evolved from some lower form of animal life into the form in which he now exists. Though still called the "*theory* of evolution," and rightly so since it has no proof and must be scientifically classified as theory only, it is presented as fact and in such a convincing manner that the student can easily be caught unaware. As was pointed out in the first lesson, we can no longer pretend that this threat does not exist, even to the juniors whom we teach. As teachers of this age group, we must be prepared to deal with this threat to their faith in the Bible account of the beginning of man. In this connection, you will want to review the points made in the first lesson concerning determining the extent to which you will need to discuss this subject in your class. The same criteria will apply here as in that lesson. You may need merely to mention the subject, or you may need to give it a fuller discussion, depending upon how much exposure to the theory of evolution your students have had.

The word "evolution" in the context in which it is used in this lesson is defined as "the theory that all species of plants and animals developed from earlier forms by hereditary transmission of slight variations in successive generations." In this lesson it is used specifically to refer to the theory which claims that man as he exists today has developed from a lower animal form. Those who believe the theory differ greatly concerning the degree of the evolutionary process; some believe that man developed from a one-celled animal, some that he came from a higher form of animal, and some even that God participated in creation but that He did not create man in the form in which he exists today. All evolutionists ultimately discredit the Genesis account of the creation of man. For further reading in this field of study, the following volumes are suggested: *The Twilight of Evolution*, by Henry Morris; *In The Beginning*, by Rita Rhodes Ward; *Evolution and Christian Faith*, by Bolton Davidheiser; *Why Scientists Accept Evolution*, by James D. Bales and Robert T. Clark.

The lesson material endeavors to present the story of the creation of man in a positive manner, building on the faith in the Bible as God's word of truth as emphasized in the first lesson. Attention is called to the differences between man and the other creations of God by discussing

Notes

the abilities which man had that other creatures did not have, the position in which God placed man, the things which he was given by God and the work that God called upon him to perform.

In the applications, the theory of evolution is introduced and identified to the students. Be sure that they understand the meaning of the word as completely as it is possible for them to do so. It may be a new word to them, even though the idea may have been presented to them at school or in something which they have seen, read, or heard. Many of the popular television cartoon programs designed for children contain evolutionary implications, as do many of the books sold for children's reading. Most of these media do not use the word "evolution," but the child should learn the word and understand it well enough to identify evolutionary ideas when he hears them.

Again God as the creator is emphasized and the warning is repeated to the child that there will be teachers and text books that will tell him that man was not made by God as the Bible account of creation states. Some simple concepts of evidences are used; the differences between man and other creatures are emphasized, and the point is made that all of these things are said of man on the day that he was created. The order of creation is discussed, showing that man was created only after God had prepared a world suitable for his habitation. You will no doubt want to add some examples of your own to emphasize these concepts.

The second application is devoted to the fact that man was created in God's image. This necessarily implies a discussion of the soul which can be a difficult concept for the juniors, particularly the younger ones in this category. The lesson emphasizes the soul as the part of man that thinks, feels, wills, and discerns right from wrong. You will need to spend considerable time on this subject adding examples of your own to give the children as much understanding of the soul as is possible at this age. The lesson endeavors to impress the student with the importance of the soul in order to help him develop early a consciousness of the necessity of learning and choosing right from wrong. Many of the older juniors are thinking seriously about obeying the gospel and are extremely aware and anxious to develop a greater understanding of the soul and of things spiritual. You can help them greatly as they search for on understanding of a concept still difficult and somewhat mysterious to them.

The exercises for this lesson include a question which calls for use of a concordance or an on-line Bible. Be sure that your students understand how to use a concordance or on-line Bible and that they have access to one.

"And the Lord God formed man of the dust of the ground, and breathed into his nostrils the breath of life; and man became a living being" (Gen. 2:7). This is a thrilling and wonderful truth. God's revelation states it in such simple terms, yet it is profound almost beyond our comprehension. It is essential that the children catch a glimpse of the glory of this marvelous truth. As a teacher, you must give your best effort to make them feel the special significance of the moment when man became a living soul.

For Lessons 2-5: Collage activities may be used again with these lessons depicting families, troubling times, and strife. You could also bring in a poster board and draw a line down the middle, dividing it in half. On one half, the words "With Sin" could be written, and on the other side, the words "Without Sin" could be written. Ask students to find faces of people in magazines depicting feelings which may display those "with sin" in their lives (anger, unhappiness, wrongdoing, criminals, etc.) and those which may display those "without sin" (happiness, love, forgiveness, making good choices, etc.).

Notes

Notes

LESSON 3

The Beginning of the Family

The lesson of the creation of Eve and the beginning of the family departs from the emphasis on the actual creation to the beginning of human relationships, the beginning of the family. In the lesson story, the creation of Eve is told, pointing out the difference in the process of her creation; she was not created from dust, but from the bone and flesh of Adam. This creation is, of course, no less a miracle than the creation of Adam, but it is different in a way that emphasizes the unity of the man and woman through which God established the family, or the home as we more often refer to it. Emphasis is given to Adam's need for a companion and the fact that no mate for him was found among the animals which God had created. No animal "evolved" into a suitable companion, nor did God expect such a process to take place. Seeing Adam's need for a companion, He purposed to create one. Nothing that He had made previously was or ever would be a suitable mate for Adam. This point, emphasized, can be an effective denial of evolutionary teaching in addition to that presented in the first and second lessons. A short while may be spent on it, if you determine that your class needs this additional rebuttal of evolution, before the lesson proceeds to other aspects.

Several terms are used in the lesson which may be in the fringe area of the junior's vocabulary, but it is almost impossible to present this material without using them. There seems to be no synonyms that express adequately the ideas which these words convey. Such words are "companion," "suitable," and "relationship." Be sure that the children have an understanding of these words as you proceed with the lesson. Sometimes they may have a vague idea of the meaning of a word, which they have heard used over and over, but the real meaning may elude them. Because of their lack of understanding of terms, a child can miss the entire import of a lesson. This would apply to any word that you feel the child may not understand. Take the time to be certain that the terms are understood. Illustrations will help as much or more than definitions. Test the child's knowledge of the word by asking him for an illustration or by asking him questions that require his understanding of the term in order for him to answer. In this way, you will know if you have communicated the meaning to him.

The lesson story as well as the applications discuss the beginning of marriage and the family, God's first laws concerning marriage, and some New Testament references to these laws. Since the next lesson concerns the beginning of sin and the next the story of Cain and Abel from the viewpoint of the strife between them, some laws of the relationships of children and parents are included in this lesson. Even though the lesson text does not include the birth of Cain and Abel, it seems appropriate to discuss the parent-children relationship in connection with the beginning of the family. It seems profitable to discuss the New Testament verses that relate to these relationships, emphasiz-

Notes

ing to the children that these are God's laws for us today. At this age the juniors may be easily embarrassed at a discussion that suggests to them a boy-girl relationship. Because of this, try to make the discussion impersonal as far as their future relationships are concerned; dwell on their knowledge of the home in which they now live. They are, after all, still looking at this lesson from a child's point of view. On the other hand, they are certainly not too young to learn God's basic laws concerning marriage and the family. The teaching of God's principles and laws on this subject will instill in them a respect for His will and a better understanding of these relationships which will be of great benefit to them when they are old enough to contemplate their own marriages and homes.

The lesson of respect for parental authority is sorely needed. The attitude toward this authority is of great importance in the child's life and in the life of the adult whom he will become. It ultimately can determine the saving of his soul. The child, who does not learn discipline and respect for authority in the home, will most likely lack respect for the authority of his teachers at school. If the pattern continues, later in life he will fail to respect the laws of his government and the society in which he lives. Ultimately he may well fail to have respect for God's authority and may lose his soul for lack of obedience to God's commands and respect for the authority of God's word. All of these possibilities should be kept in mind as you strive to impress your class with the importance of God's teaching concerning family relationships, and particularly those teachings pertaining to respect for and attitude toward authority.

In conclusion, the lesson story summarizes God's creation, its conclusion, and God's rest on the seventh day. As time permits you may want to pursue the study of the day of rest as it was set aside in the Law of Moses, commemorating God's creation, in contrast with our day of worship, commemorating the resurrection of Christ. The completeness of God's creation in emphasized in Genesis 2:1-3. This is a further indication of God's overall plan for creation.

Some parts of this lesson may be difficult to get across to the juniors, but patient effort on your part will help instill in the hearts of these children principles that can have a profound effect on their lives for years to come.

Notes

LESSON 4

The Beginning of Sin

The scope of the lesson on the beginning of sin is so vast that it is impossible to cover it in one lesson. In addition to this, it is a difficult lesson to present to this age group. The implications of the sin of Adam and Eve challenge the thinking of the most mature Bible student. It ultimately implies a discussion of God's entire scheme of redemption. The sin that came into the world when Adam and Eve disobeyed set in motion the chain of events that make up the entire history of man's relationship to God and God's plan for saving man from sin. It is the theme of the entire Bible.

In order to capture the basic teaching of the lesson for this age group, the lesson presentation is given in a simple narrative form. An effort has been made to impress the child with the fact that Adam and Eve disobeyed God's instructions, that this was sin, and that God punished them for it. If these basic ideas can be sufficiently impressed on the child's mind, they can form a foundation for a later, more complete understanding of the salvation of man from sin. Some points have been omitted but can be discussed at your discretion in view of the particular students you teach. The import of the knowledge that came to Adam and Eve as a result of eating the fruit of the tree of the knowledge of good and evil is a difficult point. The discussion of Adam and Eve's realization of their nakedness and their shame because of it can be embarrassing to this age child. Remember this and judge the appropriateness of this part of the story for yourself considering the individual children you teach.

The applications endeavor to direct the child's thinking into somewhat deeper aspects of the nature of sin than the basic facts of the story would do. They also try to relate sin to his own experience. In order to grasp this, the child needs to understand some terms. Again, these are words he probably has heard many times and thinks he knows; but they may be in the fringe area of his vocabulary. Be sure he understands them. The words "tempt" and "temptation" are two of these. The definition is given, but it may be difficult for your younger juniors. The three avenues of temptation are given and a practical example is used to help them understand. You will want to add some of your own examples. In listing the avenues of temptation, the appetite for food has been used for the biblical category of "the lust of the flesh." This is the human appetite which the children best understand. They are too young to comprehend fleshly lusts and other human appetites which adults recognize as avenues of temptation. To be sure that the children understand the idea of temptation, ask them to give you examples of things that tempt them to do wrong. Have them identify the avenue or avenues through which it tempts them. The temptation of Eve is identified for them and the suggestion is made that they study the temptation of Jesus. See if they can classify the avenues of His temptation. The understanding of temptation may be difficult

Notes

for them, but your patience in helping them will be rewarded by their increased knowledge.

The second application endeavors to identify sin and suggests what adults commonly call sins of *omission* and *commission*. The word "sin" is another term that needs to be clearly defined for the children. The examples of Adam and Eve, Jonah, and the Ten Commandments are used. You will want to use additional examples of these two classifications of sin. The idea that God will punish sin is also included.

The third application suggests God's plan for the ultimate saving of man from his sins. The love that God has for man is shown as the reason for sending His Son to make a way whereby sin can be forgiven. An appeal is made to the children to return the love that God has shown to man by obeying His commandments. At this point, you will need to determine to what extent you should discuss God's scheme of redemption. If you teach the older juniors, they can understand much of it; many of them are seriously considering obeying the gospel. If your class is made up of all of the juniors (grades 4-6), you will need to direct your efforts more generally in the direction of understanding the basic facts of God's love in preparing a way for forgiveness of sins.

Even though the lesson is difficult, your efforts in presenting it will not be in vain. You will lay a basic foundation for later understanding of God's dealing with man's sins.

Notes

LESSON 5

The Beginning of Strife

The story of the strife between Cain and Abel is probably familiar to your students, but there are many lessons to be learned from it. In the lesson story, attention is given to the matter of what was wrong with Cain's sacrifice. As pointed out, the Bible does not specify the error. Many have concluded that he offered the wrong sacrifice and have based this conclusion on the fact that, throughout the Old Testament, God required animal sacrifices and attached significance to the blood. This points to the sacrifice of Christ in which His blood was shed for the sins of all mankind. This is perhaps a valid point in studying the sacrifice of Cain; however, there are other possibilities as to the error of his offering. He could have offered his sacrifice in the wrong way, at the wrong time, at the wrong place, or with the wrong attitude. The important point for emphasis to the students is that Cain failed to do as God instructed him and this was sin.

In the discussion of this point, the New Testament verses pertaining to Abel's sacrifice are used (Rom. 10:17; Heb. 11:4). It is important that your students see the connection between these verses. Up to this point children have depended upon memory as their main method of learning, and they are just beginning to use logic. It is good for them to learn to connect two verses and draw the obvious conclusion. If faith comes by hearing and Abel offered by faith, then Abel heard God's instructions. Try some examples of this kind of reasoning with the children. For instance, if Susan went to town with her sister and Sharon is her only sister, then Susan went to town with Sharon. You will think of other examples to use.

An effort has been made to show the chain of events as Cain moved from one sin to another. He disobeyed God's instructions concerning the sacrifice, then he became angry because God refused his offering. He turned his anger, mixed with jealousy and envy, toward Abel who was not to blame in any way. This anger and jealousy led him to murder his brother; finally, he lied to God about Abel's whereabouts. Underneath all of these sinful acts is an attitude that was wrong. The same attitude that caused Cain to disrespect God's instructions concerning the sacrifice also led him into the other sins. The juniors whom you teach are old enough to begin to understand attitudes and the consequences of good and bad attitudes. This lesson provides a wonderful opportunity to show what can be the ultimate result of a wrong attitude.

The first application is directed toward an understanding of the importance of obeying God's instructions. It does not intend to imply that a Christian is not supposed to reason, but it does emphasize the error of substituting man's reasoning and ideas for God's commands and instructions. There are so many examples of this in the religions of our day; there are likewise many Bible examples of this principle. The example of Saul and the Amalekites is used because it gives such emphasis to this point. Some class time could well be spent in further study of this story.

The second application emphasizes attitude by discussing Cain's anger because of God's rejection of his sacrifice. The all-too-frequent reaction of anger toward others because of our own mistakes is pointed out. Try to get the children to talk about this as they see it in their own experiences so that they can learn to avoid this dangerous reaction. Other attitudes of Cain can be discussed as time allows.

The third application endeavors to teach the need of caring for others and of feeling a responsibility for the well-being of others. The story which Jesus told of the good Samaritan teaches this lesson so forcefully; the story of the beautiful friendship between David and Jonathan is appealing to children of this age, because they are beginning to develop deeper friendships with children their own age. Each child should learn what it means to be his brother's keeper, and the importance of feeling a responsibility for the well-being of others.

This lesson of Cain and Abel has many practical applications from which your juniors can benefit. You can make a deep and lasting impression on them by leading them to understand the errors in Cain's life and the contrasting attitudes of respect for God's commands and concern for others.

Notes

Notes

LESSON 6

A New Beginning

No story in all the Bible is any more familiar to children than the story of Noah and the ark. Most of them learned to say that Noah built the ark by the time they could say the word "Noah." Because of this the juniors may sometimes approach this lesson with an attitude of, "I know all about this already." To avoid this, you must approach the lesson with enthusiasm and present some challenging thoughts concerning a story already basically familiar to your students.

To present some thoughts that may be new to this age group, considerable space has been given to the idea of why God brought the flood. The Bible says that the people of the earth were so wicked that even the thoughts of their hearts were only wicked continually. Reflect upon the extreme degree of wickedness when everyone's thoughts were only wicked. The Genesis account says that Noah's generation was so wicked that God repented that He had even made man. Discuss how this compares with our world of today. There are people today who think good thoughts and are righteous, even though the wickedness of our generation is sometimes appalling.

The lesson reading is lengthy, but it is necessary to include this much material in order to cover the story. Insist that your students read it all; it is not difficult reading. The lesson story omits a number of facts about the ark that are included in the exercises. This is designed to make it necessary for the student to read the text in order to answer all of the questions.

The applications try to call attention to practical lessons for the students. The first application is devoted to a further discussion of the wickedness of Noah's generation, but emphasizes the fact that God took note of Noah, a single righteous man, in an entire world of evil men. Some wonderful things are said about Noah. The record says he was a just and righteous man who walked with God. How unusual this is in a world as wicked as the one described. Of utmost importance is the fact that God saw Noah's righteousness even though he was surrounded with wickedness almost beyond imagination. This is a powerful lesson in encouraging righteousness in any generation, no matter how wicked. The world does not become so evil that God does not see a righteous man. Try to help the children see this principle in their lives. When presented forcefully, it can be a great help in encouraging them to do what they have learned is right, no matter what their friends are doing.

The second application begins the lesson about faith which will be emphasized repeatedly as we study Abraham and other great Old Testament examples of faith. This application tries to define faith by giving a description of what it caused Noah to do. "Faith" is perhaps one of the words which the juniors may understand only vaguely. The younger ones may need help with it, and it is hoped that this lesson can aid their understanding. Take a little time to see how well they understand.

Some of the trials of faith are indicated in the suggestion that perhaps Noah had discouragements other than the difficulty of the work of building the ark. Here is a good place to talk about the size of the ark. A comparison that is meaningful to the children can be made between the size of the ark and a football field. If our understanding of a cubit is correct (18 inches), the ark was four hundred and fifty feet long. That is as long as 1.5 football fields. This comparison usually gets the children's attention quickly. Most of them have never realized just how big the ark was and what an undertaking it was to build it. Certainly Noah had discouragements. The suggestion is made that perhaps he was ridiculed for building such a large boat and for believing that a great flood would destroy the earth. After all, no one ever saw such a flood before. Your juniors are at the age when ridicule is a very painful experience to them. Try to make them see that Noah's faith was strong enough to carry him through all kinds of discouragements. This will help them have a better comprehension of faith and will strengthen their faith to do what they have learned is right, regardless of what others may say to them.

Using the measurements given in this lesson, help the children convert the size of the ark into something that is familiar to them today. Make a "hardware store" list of building materials; be very specific, as no substitutions would be accepted! Compare the building materials list to a recipe—can we substitute cornstarch for flour when making cookies? Why not? Discuss why it is important that we not make substitutions when God gives us instructions.

This is such an important lesson to children of this age and you will do them a great service by presenting it well.

Notes

Notes

LESSON 7

The Beginning of the Nations

The lesson text completes the story of the ark, telling of the exodus from the ark and the reestablishing of people upon the earth. It also covers the story of the tower of Babel. These two portions relate to each other in that they tell the story of the repopulating of the earth after the flood. As the original population of the earth came from Adam and Eve, the re-population of the earth after the flood came from the family of Noah. There are a number of parallels between the two stories. God told Adam to be fruitful, multiply, and replenish the earth. He repeated these exact commands to Noah (Gen. 1:28; 9:1). Noah was given dominion over all the animals as was Adam (Gen. 1:28; 9:2). These and other such comparisons again confirm the overall plan of God and the creation of man, rather than the evolution of man. Once again, in the newly cleansed earth, God sets man over the animals and shows him to be a creation of God different from all others. Again it is said that man is made in the image of God (Gen. 9:6). This is a good time to review some of the points made in lesson two concerning the creation of man as opposed to the theory of evolution. This lesson serves to reemphasize the points made in that lesson.

Just as there was sin in the lives of the sons of Adam, so there was sin in the new world in the lives of the sons of Noah. This is not mentioned in the lesson text since it is somewhat of a departure from the line of thought pertaining to the development of the nations. But certainly it can be considered, if class time allows. It is interesting to note the descendants of Canaan (Ham's son) as mentioned in Genesis 10. There are many mentioned in this chapter that reappear frequently in the history of the Israelites. The Canaanites, the Jebusites, the Amorites, and the Hivites are some of the ones most frequently mentioned.

In the story of the tower of Babel, we find the actual scattering of the people to form the nations of the earth. This story, often overlooked in a study such as this, and more often given only a brief mention, has a number of ideas that are important. The lesson application that refers to this attempts to point out that it is an example of an addition to God's commands as well as a substitution. The entire effort of the building of the tower was a rejection of that which God had told Noah and his descendants to accomplish, that is to multiply and replenish the earth. The tower was intended to be a means of keeping the people from scattering to replenish the earth. Their purpose was to do the opposite from God's commands, and they endeavored to accomplish it by adding something that God had said nothing about. The people set as their goals building a tower that would reach to heaven and building themselves a name, lest they be scattered over the earth. God saw that, if He allowed this to be accomplished, man would continue to do whatever he imagined, adding and substituting with nothing restrained. As God had placed a barrier before the garden of Eden to keep Adam and Eve from eating the fruit of the tree of life and thus living forever, so here He confuses the language to prevent man from doing that which was not in His plan for mankind. He thus expresses His disapproval of man's additions and substitutions for His commands. To help the children see the error of adding to God's word, two simple suggestions are made concerning the construction of the ark. You will no doubt think of other examples that you may wish to include. This discussion provides an excellent opportunity to show how this principle applies to the religious denominations of today. Your students will be able to mention many additions that they have observed, heard about, or learned about from their friends. Involve them in the discussion as much as time allows.

The other application concerns the serious consideration that should be given to the making and breaking of promises. The promise God made to Noah and confirmed by the sign of the rainbow is an excellent example to use. The lesson emphasizes the fact that God's promises are always true and that He never breaks or forgets a promise. They are encouraged to take the perfect example of God's promises as an incentive for learning the importance of their own promises, and the necessity of care in both making and keeping them. The Bible is abundant in examples of God's promises. This lesson uses a reference to God's promise to destroy the Amalekites. Review this story carefully or use other Bible examples as you prefer. If time allows have the children find examples and be prepared to relate them in class.

In this generation when we see a complete disregard for promises made and for the validity of a man's word, this seems to be a most important and significant principle to impress upon the children whom you teach.

If time allows, make a recipe substituting an ingredient you discussed in a previous lesson (keep the recipe simple). Show the students that one simple substitution can make a huge difference and that it is very important to follow the instructions as given. It is the same as the instructions that God gives us and we must not change the instructions He has given us.

Notes

Notes

LESSON 8

The Beginning of a Special Nation (1)

These lessons begin to study the character traits found in Abraham and the promises that God made to him. Instill the character traits of obedience and faithfulness in students in these two lessons by focusing on what these words mean and how they are shown.

The story of Abraham covers twelve chapters of the book of Genesis, but only two of the lessons of this book are devoted to it. This means that much of the material in the Bible account of Abraham must be omitted. However, an effort has been made to incorporate the high points of the story of Abraham. Though the reading is too lengthy to require of the children, you should read the entire story and be ready to supplement the lesson story as your time may allow.

In keeping with the title of the lesson, "The Beginning of a Special Nation," the promises made to Abraham are discussed in the beginning of the lesson, and the story is told with an emphasis on the fulfillment of these promises. Though the promises are sometimes listed and presented as some seven or eight different ones, it seems easier for the juniors to remember the four basic areas of promises as given in the lesson. These are the promises of great material blessings, a son, a nation, and a blessing to all mankind. They can be reduced to four words for ease of memory: riches, son, nation, and Christ. The first two of these are of course fulfilled in Abraham's lifetime, and are pointed out in this and the following lesson. The second two are not fulfilled in this book, so an effort should be made to emphasize them enough that the children will remember them and be aware of their fulfillment as they study other books of this series. The promise of a great nation is fulfilled in the giving of the law which established Israel as the chosen people of God and in the possession of the land under Joshua. The promise that the seed of Abraham would be a blessing to all mankind is fulfilled in the coming of Christ and the subsequent establishment of the New Testament church through which all men can receive salvation.

The story of Lot is included because it tells of the fulfillment of the promise of material blessings. It is also an excellent example of selfishness on the part of Lot and of unselfishness on the part of Abraham. This is further emphasized in the applications. The story of the birth of Ishmael is also included since it has a direct bearing on the promise of a son and the promises pertaining to the seed of Abraham. You will want to add as much of this material as time will allow.

The applications both in this lesson and in the following lesson list some of the qualities of Abraham that made him one of the outstanding men in the Bible. It is suggested to the children that these are perhaps the reasons why God chose Abraham to be the father of His chosen people.

The underlying quality of all of the ones listed would be the great faith of Abraham. Called the father of the faithful, Abraham exemplified faith in God in almost everything that he did. Since the lesson of Noah discussed the example of faith in some detail, the applications in this lesson mention the great faith of Abraham and then use some of the other noble qualities in the life of Abraham as examples to the children for their own lives. This does not minimize the great faith of Abraham, and you should be sure that your students understand that in Abraham is found one of the greatest examples of faith anywhere.

The qualities of Abraham used in this lesson are obedience, courage, and unselfishness. The principle of obedience, as exemplified in the life of Abraham, is sorely needed today. In an age where obedience and respect for authority are scorned on every hand, there is an urgency to emphasize the true spirit of obedience. The child who has not learned to obey his parents in the home, will not obey his teachers in school. If he does not learn obedience at this level, he will not learn obedience to the laws of the land, and will ultimately fail in his obedience to God. The pattern of a true spirit of obedience must be set in the very young child if we expect him to be willing to obey God when he is a mature individual. This lesson of obedience should be emphasized as strongly as possible.

The quality of courage is likewise needed today. Though the things asked of us today are not the some as those asked of Abraham, he becomes a wonderful example to us of a man who had the courage to do as God asked. The children whom you teach have probably already experienced situations in which they have found it difficult to do what they have learned is right. It takes courage to stand for one's convictions in the face of temptations and ridicule. It takes much less courage to do what the crowd does. Try to make this point clear to the children and help them look to Abraham and other Bible characters as examples of courage in doing God's will and in standing for right.

Abraham's unselfishness is another of his good qualities. God had promised him great material blessings and had made him "very rich in cattle, in silver, and in gold." So often, one who has been blessed with riches becomes selfish and greedy, trusting in his riches rather than in God. Abraham is a wonderful example of one who did not have this attitude toward his riches. When the herdsmen of Abraham and Lot quarreled over the land, Abraham suggested that they separate their flocks so there would be no strife between them. Abraham gave Lot the choice of the land. Certainly this is an example of the unselfishness of Abraham, just as Lot's example is one of extreme selfishness. Lot failed to consider that Abraham had brought him to this land, had treated him as a son, and had given him what he now had. Lot selfishly chose the best for himself. God was pleased with Abraham's attitude and rewarded him for his unselfishness. This story is an excellent one for the children to learn and should be emphasized strongly.

Notes

Notes

LESSON 9

The Beginning of a Special Nation (2)

The continuation of the story of Abraham and of God's great promises to him is the subject of this lesson. The story of the birth of Isaac is told with emphasis upon the fact that this is a fulfillment of one of the promises made to Abraham. You will want to take some time to explain that Isaac was the seed of Abraham and that, through him, the other promises of God to Abraham would be fulfilled. The nation of Israel would come through Isaac, and likewise Christ should come from the seed of Abraham through Isaac. This is a good time to look at this promise as it passed from Abraham to Isaac, to Jacob, etc. The following simple chart may help:

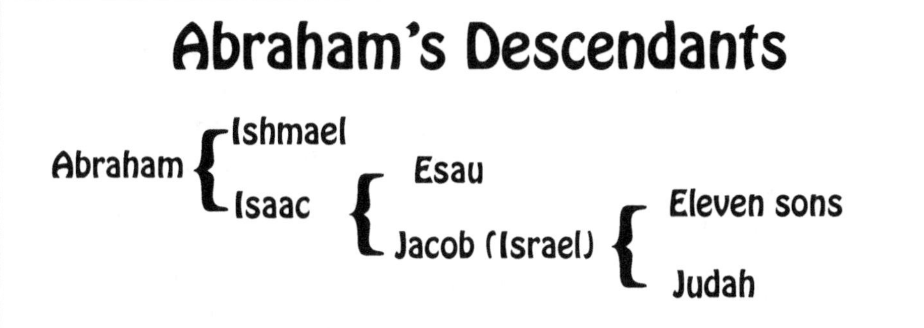

The descendants of the twelve sons became the nation of Israel. Christ came through Judah, the fourth son.

Since there were two basic areas of the promise that were not fulfilled in Abraham's lifetime, they are passed from one generation to the next and are identified as "the promise" as given from Abraham to Isaac, from Isaac to Jacob, etc. The promise of the nation is fulfilled in the descendants of Jacob (Israel). The tribes that were the descendants of the twelve sons of Jacob made up the nation of Israel who received the law of God in the wilderness, possessed the land under Joshua, and became the kingdom of Israel under Saul, David, and Solomon. The promise of the blessings to all families of earth was passed from Jacob to his fourth son, Judah, and it was from his tribe that Christ was born many centuries later. Take the time to give this considerable emphasis so that the children will be aware of these promises and their fulfillment as they study the Old Testament further. There is great significance in the story of Abraham as the beginning of the unfolding of God's scheme of redemption for all mankind. The children you teach can understand much of this and it is important to lay this foundation at this point in their study.

There is a departure from the thread of the promises to tell the remainder of the story of Lot. It seems an excellent time to point out the ultimate fate of a selfish man. Certainly the final picture we have of Lot is a vastly different one from the properous man whom Abraham brought from Ur as one of his family. The point is also made that God was displeased with the extreme wickedness of Sodom and Gomorrah and destroyed the cities because of it.

The final segment of the lesson story tells the incident of Abraham's being called upon to offer Isaac as a sacrifice. Certainly this is a wonderful example of faith and should be emphasized. The command to offer the cherished son of his old age, the promised child, as a sacrifice to God must have been a grievous thing to Abraham. We know that God considered it the great test of Abraham's faith because of the statement of the angel when he commanded Abraham to lay not his hand upon Isaac. There is no more beautiful language to be found anywhere in the Bible:

> By Myself I have sworn, says the Lord, because you have done this thing, and have not withheld your son, your only son—blessing I will bless you, and multiplying I will multiply your descendants as the stars of the heaven and as the sand which is on the seashore; and your descendants shall possess the gate of their enemies. In your seed all the nations of the earth shall be blessed, because you have obeyed My voice (Gen. 22:16-18).

The writer of Hebrews (11:17-19) tells us that Abraham offered Isaac, his only begotton son, who was to be his seed as God had promised. Abraham believed that God was able to raise Isaac up from the dead if necessary. What a great example of faith this is for us. Juniors will appreciate it if you impress them with the impact of this story of Abraham's great faith.

The applications consider two more of the qualities of Abraham that made him a man who pleased God. Abraham's hospitality and generosity are seen many times in his story, and especially in the incident of his entertaining the strangers. Very closely connected with this is Abraham's love and concern for his family as suggested in the second application. You will probably think of other incidents in his life as revealed to us that exemplify these and other desirable traits in this man.

In the study of Abraham we certainly find one of the great men of the Bible. A careful study of Abraham can be inspiring to your students as they see in him so many reasons why God chose him from among all the men of the earth to be the father of His chosen people.

Notes

Notes

LESSON 10

Isaac

The story of Isaac is one often skipped or given little attention in the study of the book of Genesis. There is much less told about Isaac than about some of the other patriarchs, but there are some important lessons to be learned from his story. The son of a famous father and the father of a famous son, Isaac stands suspended between Abraham, one of the greatest men in all the Bible, and Jacob, one of the most colorful and dynamic personalities we read about in Scripture. Because of this and because Isaac had a vastly different personality from either of the other two, he is often passed over lightly or considered a weak or uninteresting person in a study of the great men of Genesis.

However, there seems to be some important lessons to learn from the man Isaac. He was a quiet, peaceful man. His example of doing good to others is outstanding. God saw these qualities and rewarded him with great riches and prosperity.

In the lesson story, emphasis is given to the story of the selection of Isaac's wife, Rebekah. This is an interesting and fascinating story to children of this age. The manner in which a wife was selected in that day was so different from the way in which it is done in our present-day, western culture that it becomes interesting from this point of view, also. The story of Isaac's dealing with the Philistines when he went to live in the part of the land inhabited by them is given rather careful attention for it was in this story that we see some of the traits in Isaac that distinguish him from other men of his time and that are important in making a study of him practical and significant to us.

Attention is also given to the promise as it was passed from Abraham to Isaac. Since two of God's promises were not fulfilled in Abraham's lifetime, Abraham passed them down to Isaac and God reaffirmed them to Isaac. Once again, God says that He will make a great nation of the seed of Abraham and the seed of Isaac. Once again, He promises to bless all the nations of earth through this seed. It is important that the children understand the passing of this promise, for it will play a significant part in the life of Jacob.

The applications draw lessons for the children today from the character traits of Isaac that made him outstanding. Isaac was a peaceful man and he returned good for evil. When he moved to the land of the Philistines because of the famine, he encountered hostility from them. In order to provide for his large flocks and herds and for the people of his household, it was necessary for him to have water for them. He immediately set about cleaning the wells that had belonged to his father Abraham, but which the Philistines had filled. When the Philistines took two of these wells from him, each time he did not fight them for the wells, but moved to another location and cleaned out or dug another well. In this action, Isaac exemplified one of the great traits of his character. He refused to be involved in a fight with the Philistines

Notes

over a well. Many would say that Isaac had a weakness of character because he would not fight for what was his. Certainly he could have. Abraham had raised an army from his own servants to deliver Lot in the early days of their sojourn in Canaan. Isaac was a rich man, and no doubt could have fought for the wells had he desired. But this was not Isaac's nature. He was a man of peace. By not fighting, and by being concerned over his household and about the care and prosperity of it, he won a more lasting good will from the Philistines. They observed that, though he did not fight them for his wells, he prospered and was a great and rich man among them. It was their conclusion that the Lord was with Isaac, and they sought to make a covenant with him. When they came to Isaac to make the covenant, he greeted them with hospitality and kindness. Such a spirit of returning good for evil made the encounter successful and established peace and good will with the Philistines. Though Isaac could probably have fought successfully for the wells, the attitude of the Philistines would have remained hostile. The attitude and example of nonretaliation in Isaac won for him a peace that no battle could have won.

In our age, when the attitude is often one of "I'll take what's mine no matter what I have to do," or "I won't be treated this way," the attitude of Isaac is a refreshing example of a man who looked beyond the immediate situation to a solution that was ultimately better for his own household, won the friendship and respect of his neighbors, and certainly was pleasing to God. Try to make a lasting impression on the children of this noble spirit of peace in Isaac. It is a character trait that is much needed in our world of violence and hostility.

The last three lessons focus on additional character traits of Isaac, Jacob, Esau, and Joseph. Again, discuss with the students which traits they see in each of these men (good and bad), and discuss how we can apply them in our lives. Are these traits God approved? How can we work on these traits? How can we help others work on these traits?

As with all lessons, we want the students to commit their memory verses to memory. Ask the students to write out the lesson's memory verse on a 3 x 5 index card. Book rings may be purchased and the index cards may be put onto the book rings each class period after a hole is punched into the card. This will be a good way for the students to collect the memory verses and review them each time you meet.

Notes

LESSON 11

Jacob and Esau

In the story of Jacob we study one of the most colorful of all the Old Testament characters. Jacob's life is filled with events that are both interesting and teachable to the juniors. The lesson story deals first with the relationships in the family of Isaac, calling attention to Esau as Isaac's favorite and Jacob as Rebekah's. The birthright and the promise are discussed along with Jacob's methods of obtaining both. Be sure that your students understand both the birthright and the promise and are able to distinguish between them. Sometimes they are confused on this point.

The second section of the lesson story tells of Jacob's sojourn in Haran and the obtaining of his wives. Because of space limitation, the story of Jacob's dream has been omitted (Gen. 28:10-22). It should be pointed out that God's promise to Jacob is the continuation of the promise which God made to Abraham (Gen. 28:14). There are many details of Jacob's relationship with Laban and his departure from Haran which have been omitted, but which can be included profitably if time permits. The story of Jacob's later life, after his return to his original home, is included in the next lesson on the life of Joseph.

The first application of the lesson discusses God's law of sowing and reaping. The full meaning of this principle may elude the juniors unless you are careful to help them understand it. However, it is most important that they learn this principle, and there is no better example of it than Jacob's life. An example from nature is included, and you will no doubt think of other examples that can help them understand the practical implications of this law. It is important to relate it to your students' lives and to urge them to give you examples that they have observed.

The second application deals with the development of a proper sense of values. In our materialistic society the meaningful values of life, particularly spiritual values, are often overlooked in the emphasis on material things. Young people need to be taught to look ahead and to discern those things that are ultimately valuable to their happiness and to their spiritual well-being. Esau is an outstanding example of a man who made a choice with no regard for real value. Though his choice was between two material items, his disregard of the great value of his birthright is a most vivid example of a man who failed to appreciate that which he had that was of true value and who could not see beyond his momentary distress to that which was ultimately in his best interest. God said he despised his birthright because he exchanged it for something of lesser value.

The story of the great choice of Moses and Christ's reference to the hidden treasure and the pearl of great price are also mentioned and should be emphasized. The students will probably be quick to remember some bad choices they have observed.

The lessons of sowing and reaping and of developing a sense of true and lasting values are important and you will benefit your students greatly if you can help them to better understand both of these great principles.

Notes

Notes

LESSON 12

Joseph

The story of Joseph is lengthy, covering thirteen chapters of the book of Genesis (37; 39-50). It is important for the teacher to read this entire text carefully before presenting the material to the class so that the facts of the story are firmly fixed in his mind. Children of this age are inquisitive about the minute details of this kind of story and will be interested in the fine points of it. Read the entire story before presenting the first lesson, since there are two lessons devoted to the story of Joseph.

Joseph is one of the few major Bible characters about whom we are told nothing bad. Unless the instance of his hiding the cup in Benjamin's sack is construed to be deceitful, there is no sin of his recorded. Of course he was not a perfect individual, but the fact that no wrong doing is recorded would indicate that, in his example, there are many lessons to be learned. Joseph was a young man in most of the story, and his story is, consequently, appealing to young people.

There are many applications to be drawn from Joseph's life. They are among the easiest to emphasize to juniors; they are also of great importance to them. If the facts of the story are fairly familiar to your class, a considerable amount of time can be spent on the applications. The four used in this lesson seem to be of primary importance.

1. Beware of hatred. Hatred is a sinister emotion and one which is displayed before young people on every hand. It is not the nature of children to hate, but today they are learning it at an early age. Through entertainment media, they see violence, disregard of human life, rebellion, and lack of respect for authority. At school, they hear their classmates echo expressions of prejudice and hatred learned from their parents. This must be counteracted. This lesson offers a good opportunity to show the fruits of hatred. Show that hatred actually led Joseph's brothers to be willing to kill their own brother. The teaching of Jesus on hatred is of particular importance in this lesson, since He showed the direct relationship of hatred and murder (Matt. 5:21-22; 1 John 3:15). His teaching about loving one's enemy should be included in this discussion (Matt. 5:44). Let the children give you an example of someone who has treated them badly and then show that the teaching of Jesus tells them to return to that person a kindness in exchange for the unkindness. Assure them that they will have a feeling of satisfaction and the pleasure of God after having done this. Challenge them to try it.

2. Don't be a complainer. In our affluent society it seems to be stylish to complain and gripe. This attitude is contagious, and it is rampant among young people. Though the juniors are young for it in its rankest form, they are susceptible. Joseph is an excellent example of one who, from our point of view, had every right to think that the world and God were against him; still we are not told that he ever uttered one complaint. Picture just how many catastrophic things happened to him.

A favored son of a rich man, at seventeen he suddenly found himself a slave sold by his own brothers. Taken to a strange country, he is able to make a place for himself, only to be put in prison because of lies told about him by a wicked woman because he resisted her temptations and did as God would have wished. Yet in all of this, he did not blame God or fail to trust in Him. This can make a very graphic example. Try to emphasize to the children that they have so many wonderful blessings: parents who love them, home, family, clothes, food, good schools, etc. Show them that they should be ashamed to complain about insignificant troubles in view of so many good things.

Notes

3. Do a job well. Indifference toward a job is likewise a result of our affluent society in which young people have not been taught to work and in which things have come to them too easily. Many employers say that it is almost impossible to find young people who are truly conscientious about doing a good job of their assigned tasks. Joseph did his work well. This is shown in a number of incidents in his life. When his father sent him to see how his brothers fared at Shechem, he did not find them there; but instead of returning home and saying that they weren't there, he inquired after them and followed them on to Dothan, farther to the north. As a slave in Potiphar's house, he did his work so well that he was made overseer of the house and all that Potiphar had. In prison, he was likewise soon put in charge of the other prisoners. This is characteristic of all of Joseph's life. Emphasize to the children that, by doing their chores well, they gain the gratitude of their parents, the respect of others, and the pleasure of God. Use some of the common chores that children of this age might be asked to do as examples; use some tasks that might not be so pleasant to them. Help them learn that there is pleasure and satisfaction in a task well done.

4. Do what is right no matter where you are. This application is of great importance. It is one of the finest of Joseph's examples. It is fairly easy to behave well when family and friends are watching and encouraging one to do the right thing; but when one is on his own and away from those who expect a certain standard from him, the temptation to do the wrong, momentarily advantageous, thing is great. This situation becomes the real test of conviction. These juniors are by no means too young to have strong convictions about doing what they have been taught is right, and this point should be strongly emphasized. Joseph is a classic example of one who resisted temptation and did what was pleasing to God because he had deep convictions, the willingness to stand by them, and the earnest desire to please God above all else. It is needless to say how important these principles are to young people. Use this lesson and the fine example of Joseph to make a strong, lasting impression of them.

For the older and more mature juniors there are some additional points of discussion that can be profitable and thought provoking as time and class situation permit.

1. Discuss the providence of God as shown in the life of Joseph. God used a series of seeming tragedies in the life of Joseph to bring about His will and the salvation of His chosen people from famine.

2. Discuss the result of Jacob's partiality to Joseph. Is this the attitude that set the whole chain of events into motion?

Notes

3. Discuss the attitude of Reuben and Judah in the effort to kill Joseph as contrasted to the rest of the brothers. Did they fear the wrath of Jacob if Joseph was lost? Did they care more for Joseph than the others did? Did Reuben regard the responsibility of being the oldest enough to cause him to try to save Joseph?

4. Show that the deceiving of Jacob into thinking that Joseph was dead illustrates one of God's eternal principles, "Whatsoever a man sows, that he will also reap" (Gal. 6:7). Remind the class that Jacob practiced deceit in obtaining the blessing from his father. In this story he reaps the seed of deceit.

In this lesson and the one to follow, which is also on Joseph, you have one of the best opportunities available to you as a Bible teacher to instill some of these basic principles exemplified in the life of Joseph into the lives of the young people you teach. Don't fail to take full advantage of this opportunity. Your reward will be great as you watch these children grow and as you see them put to use in their lives some of these great truths that you have helped teach them.

LESSON 13

God's People Go to Egypt

Notes

This second lesson on the life of Joseph covers a lengthy narrative found in Genesis 40 through 50. Only chapters 40 through 45 have been listed in the lesson as the Scripture to read. Even this reading is lengthy for children of this age, but they should be encouraged to read it in its entirety. It is a fascinating and interesting story and this will appeal to most of the children. Try to emphasize this point and encourage them to read the entire story as they would any interesting narrative. Arouse their curiosity and interest by suggesting just a few of the intriguing points of the story, i.e. the way that Joseph used the hiding of his cup in Benjamin's sack to assure their return.

As time permits, discuss the high points of the remaining chapters of the book of Genesis (46-50). Since this concludes the study of the book, it is well to include this material in a brief way. Some of these items are: the actual journey of Jacob down to Egypt; the meeting of Jacob and Joseph after some twenty years of separation; the introduction of Jacob and his sons to Pharaoh; Jacob's illness, death, and subsequent burial at Machpelah; Jacob's blessing to Joseph's sons and his final words to his own sons; the promise given to Judah; Joseph's death.

As in the preceeding lesson, the applications drawn from Joseph's life are emphasized. They are important and practical for children in this age group.

1. Being trustworthy. The word "trustworthy" may be a bit difficult for the younger juniors, but it is a word that they need to understand. A rather detailed definition by example has been included in the lesson text, but this may not be enough for thorough understanding. Try to use other illustrations and explanations of this characteristic. Ask the children to give you examples from their experiences. You will know from this whether or not they understand the implications of being trustworthy. Honesty in word and in handling anything belonging to another, diligence in fulfilling responsibility, and conviction in doing what is right, are all important aspects of being trustworthy. Joseph's life is a fine example of all of these characteristics. Have the class cite examples from the story of his life. Some of these are: his diligence in searching for his brothers at Dothan; his honesty in handling Potiphar's household; his refusal to sin with Potiphar's wife; his behavior in prison. His ultimate high position in Egypt is one of the results of his trustworthiness.

2 A forgiving spirit. "I'll get even with him" and "I hope he gets what's coming to him," are expressions heard too often, even among Christians. Children of this age, learning rapidly to be independent and self-sufficient, too often echo these expressions thinking them to indicate that they are growing up and learning to stand on their own feet. It is important to emphasize that this is not the attitude of one who would follow the teaching and example of Jesus. He forgave even those

Notes

who crucified Him, and taught us to love our enemies and to do good to those who hate us (Matt. 5:44). He taught His disciples to forgive seventy times seven (Matt. 18:21-22). Joseph forgave the brothers who would have killed him and who indeed did sell him into slavery. Joseph and Jesus did not wait until the offenders asked for forgiveness. Try to relate this teaching to the lives and experiences of the children you work with. Emphasize to them that, if Joseph and Jesus could forgive such great wrongs against themselves, we should certainly be able to forgive the less serious wrongs and unkindnesses directed to us. This comparison can make a lasting impression on the minds of the children.

3. God's Providence. A detailed study of the providence of God would be too involved and complicated for this age group, but they can certainly understand and appreciate the fact that God uses people and happenings to fulfill His purposes. Joseph's fate seemed terrible from a human standpoint, yet God used it as a means of saving Joseph's family and of separating them to be His chosen people. Later in the history of the Israelites, God spared the baby Moses from a death all other children like him were experiencing for His purpose of once again saving His people. Joseph believed that all of the things that befell him were used to accomplish God's purpose. He told his brothers that his being sold as a slave had been used by God as a means of saving their lives. Joseph was willing to trust God's plan and purpose. Children of this age should be taught to trust God and to understand that He will fulfill His promises.

Summary

The lessons of this quarter have attempted to survey the entire book of Genesis. As said in the beginning, this is a monumental task because of the scope of the material covered in the book. However, by this time, the juniors should have a more basic understanding of the creation, a good acquaintance with the characters whose stories are told, and a concept of the beginnings of God's chosen people and of His plan to provide salvation for all mankind. On this foundation which you have helped give them, they will be better able to understand their continued Bible study and to apply the principles taught and exemplified to their own lives. This will bring you, their teacher, a great amount of satisfaction and encouragement.

Lesson 1

Jesus Chooses His Apostles

The Aim

- To know what the word "apostle" means and the scope and the purpose of the office of an apostle.
- To feel that God's work is important and that there is something everyone can do.
- To do. Be able to tell why there are no apostles in the church today.

A man's true worth is his character. It is not how much a man owns or who he is that matters. What really counts is what he is—and that is character. Character is something that is developed and molded; its roots reach into childhood. This workbook is one of character sketches of the apostles. Character development is its main thrust. Students at this age like to study about famous people. This is a big advantage for you, the teacher. Your students should be naturally interested in what you are teaching. And besides, what you are teaching is vital. Be certain as you study the apostles to lay stress on the kind of men they were.

Some Suggestions

A good dictionary is necessary for good teaching. *The Thorndike-Barnhart Junior Dictionary* is the best. Its vocabulary is excellent. There are many one-volume editions of *Webster Dictionaries* but none is as good as the Thorndike-Barnhart series. The value of the *Webster Dictionary* lies in the large unabridged edition; here the *Webster Dictionary* is the Supreme Court in its field. Have the student use the dictionary when the meaning of a word is not clear or is not known.

The Master's Men by William Barclay may also prove to be helpful. It is available in a paperback edition and is rather inexpensive. Barclay is a lucid writer, but his treatment on the traditions and legends of the apostles is rather fanciful. If you have no other book on the apostles, it's worth the price. Any Bible encyclopedia will have entries on the Apostles and and the individual apostles.

Another suggestion is to make a large chart on the apostles. This will help both the teaching and the learning. One picture is worth a thousand words! Keep reviewing the chart with the students. Below is a sample chart. Lesson 4 should explain any questions you might have.

SIMON PETER
Andrew, James, John

PHILIP
Nathanael (Bartholomew),
Levi (Matthew), Thomas

JAMES THE LESS
Judas (Thaddaeus, Lebbaeus),
Simon the Zealot, Judas Iscariot

Notes

Teaching Lesson 1

To explain what the word "apostle" means, you might want to sketch a ship, a letter, and two stick-men on the blackboard. Ask how each of the drawings could be called an apostle.

Another thought to emphasize is that the apostles were ordinary men. What God wants today is ordinary people doing ordinary things faithfully. This is what is important. A good question to ask would be: "What are some ordinary things we can do today?" List the answers on the black-board.

On the selection of Matthias, you will want to read from Acts 1:23-26. Show how it was the Lord who chose Matthias. Also show that Matthias did not receive a majority of votes but that only one lot fell upon him. The one thing that Matthias, the Twelve, and Paul had in common was that they were all chosen by the Lord.

A young mind may find it hard to understand why there were only twelve apostles. 'Why not six or twenty?" The last paragraph in the lesson discusses this. But don't assume that a fifth or sixth grade student will know the difference between a Jew and a Gentile. Here's an opportunity to use the dictionary. Have them give you the answer. They will remember it longer that way.

Lesson 2

Ambassadors for Christ

Notes

The Aim

- To know the apostles were ambassadors and that their authority was a delegated authority; it came from heaven.
- To feel. To respect the writings of the apostles and other inspired men because they spoke for God.
- To do. Be able to explain how the apostles were in Christ's stead or in His place.

The first law of teaching is: The teacher must know that which he would teach. That sounds simple enough but it is something that is often overlooked. In fact, most class problems arise because the teacher was not prepared to teach. He did not know his material or he had not selected a method of presentation.

What does it mean to know your material? Study your lesson and study it early. The teacher who waits until Sunday morning before he prepares will not be very effective. His class will be dull or boring. The students will not be interested and may even be unruly. The right time to prepare for any lesson is five to seven days before you teach it! Early preparation has no substitutes. Know your material and know it early.

Knowing your lesson also means selecting a method of presentation. How will you teach? Will it be all lecture? Discussion? Or will you simply cover the questions at the end of the lesson? The teacher should know where he is going and what he is going to do when he gets there. The more response you can get from your students, the better the class. A good teacher is not so much a lecturer as he is a guide. He guides his students through the lesson rather than just telling them the lesson. Ask leading questions as you go through the lesson. If possible, have the students tell you what you want them to learn. A few examples of how this is done are given below in Teaching Lesson Two. A good teacher will ask questions, lecture, channel discussion, and review all in the same lesson. This is the crux of teaching and this is its secret.

Some Suggestions

If you made the chart on the apostles as was suggested in lesson one, now is the time to use it again. Repetition is the best teacher.

Another thought is a newspaper clipping about an ambassador. If you cannot locate one, try the local library. Most libraries will have *Ambassador's Report* by Chester Bowles. There are some excellent photographs in the book on the role of an ambassador. This should make it easier to explain how the apostles were ambassadors for Christ.

Teaching Lesson 2

You will want to read 2 Corinthians 5:20 in class. The translation by Charles B. Williams may be easier for a young mind to understand: "So I am an envoy to represent Christ, because it is through me that God is

Notes

making His appeal. As one representing Christ I beg you, be reconciled to God." The points needing emphasis are: Paul was an ambassador and he represented Christ. Here is a good leading question: Why then, do you think the disciples in Thessalonia received Paul's words as the word of God (1 Thess. 2:13)?

"Delegated authority" may be something a young mind has trouble understanding. Again, use the dictionary by having a student read the definition for "delegate." Matthew 16:19 is an important text. The Charles B. Williams translation should again be helpful: "I will give you the keys of the kingdom of heaven and whatever you forbid on earth must be what is already forbidden in heaven, and whatever you permit on earth must be what is already permitted in heaven" (Italics, ours). Williams is accurate; the verb is a perfect passive participle and expresses something in a state of having been already forbidden or permitted. Peter is not telling heaven what to do—it is really the other way around. Unfortunately, the rendering of the KJV ("shall be loosed") is a little misleading. The point the students need to master is that of delegated authority. Heaven's authority was delegated to the apostles. "Why then," you might ask, "is it important that men listen to what the apostles say?" Because they speak on behalf of Christ, they are His ambassadors.

The Creative Bible Teacher

always obeys

The Seven Laws of Teaching

1. The teacher must know that which he would teach.
2. The teacher must help the student to attend with interest to the lesson being taught.
3. The teacher must teach in a language understood by the student.
4. The teacher must begin with the known and proceed to the unknown.
5. S. The teacher must excite and guide the self-activities of the student.
6. The teacher must aim at getting the student to reproduce the WORD IN THE HEART.
7. The teacher must complete, test, and confirm his work by review and application.

These laws are explained in detail in *The Seven Laws of Teaching*, by Milton Gregory.

Lesson 3

The Spirit of Truth

Notes

The Aim

- To know that the apostles were guided into all truth by the Holy Spirit.
- To feel or have confidence in the record left by the apostles and others because they were divinely inspired.
- To do. Be able to explain how the Holy Spirit was the Helper of the apostles.

Attitudes influence actions: "As he thinks in his heart, so is he" (Prov. 23:7). The way we teach is a reflection of our attitudes about teaching. It is a mirror. Effective teaching just doesn't happen. It is a result of a clear understanding of what teaching is and the principles involved.

There is nothing more important than teaching children the Scriptures. This is true because what is taught in childhood is seen in manhood and will be read in eternity. The responsibility you have as a teacher is an awesome one.

Children are naturally curious and inquisitive. They are born with enthusiasm. Unfortunately, that enthusiasm is sometimes stifled in a classroom by dull illustrations or poor preparation on the part of the teacher. Good teaching is not stuffed with facts but is filled with ideas. Good teaching inspires a student rather than puts him to sleep. A good teacher is more of a guide than a lecturer. He lectures just enough to give a sense of direction to his students. As a teacher, you will want to ask questions again and again. By doing this you will encourage your class to think and respond. This is what makes teaching enjoyable and refreshing. And this is what gives teaching life.

Patience is the golden key in teaching. The servant of the Lord must be patient (2 Tim. 2:24). Patience is especially needed when teaching young minds so fresh from God. Remember, everything is new to them. They are children—not miniature adults. But there are times when this escapes us.

We become vexed because our students are not learning as they should. When this happens, sit down and try to write with your left hand—and then remember that a child is all left hand.

Teaching Lesson 3

The following is a sample of how the author would teach lesson three. Let's say we have forty-five minutes. Our plan is to spend about one-third (or 15 minutes) of the available time in light discussion. The remaining two-thirds (or 30 minutes) will be spent in review by answering the questions in the lesson. This is how a typical class might go:

Teacher: "Our lesson this week is about the apostles. Does anyone remember what the word 'apostle' means?" No answer. Teacher: "Don't you recall in our first lesson the drawings we put on the blackboard—

Notes

the two stick-men, the letter. . . ?" A student interrupts: "Apostle means being sent." Teacher: "That's right. The apostles were sent as ambassadors of Christ, weren't they? This week we're going to talk about how the apostles were directed or guided in their work. This was done by the Holy Spirit. Let's all open our Bibles to John 13. Look especially at verse 27. What was the last thing Jesus said to Judas?" A student replies by reading the verse. Teacher: "Do you think Judas knew what Jesus meant? (Pause) And what about the other apostles? Do you think they knew Judas was leaving so he could betray Jesus?" Several in the class now respond. The teaches commends them and continues: "Do you think the apostles were sad when Jesus told them He was going to leave them?" Student: "Yes." Teacher: "How do we know?" No reply. Teacher: "Look at John 14:1. What did Jesus say about their hearts?" (Pause) The teacher continues.

The idea is briefly to cover the material and then review with the questions that appear at the end of the lesson. This way you will cover the material twice.

Lesson 4

The Master's Men

Notes

The Aim

- To know the names of the twelve apostles.
- To feel that the apostles were real men—not just some names on paper.
- To do. Be able to tell something about each of the twelve apostles.

The second law of teaching is: Teaching is only successful when the pupils attend with interest to the material being taught. This simply means that a part of teaching is getting and keeping the interest of your students. Interest is an essential ingredient in teaching. It's like flour in a cake—without it everything else flops!

This may surprise you but disinterest in a class is primarily the teacher's fault! The problem is not the "younger generation" or the subject you're studying. What we are saying is that the teacher is in a position to do something about disinterest. And because of this, he is responsible for the inattention of his students. What are some reasons for inattention or disinterest?

Poor preparation on the part of the teacher is a big reason. If the teacher does not know his material well, the pupils will lose interest. It's that simple.

Another factor may be discomfort. Extremes of temperature in a room (too hot or too cold) and poor ventilation are two sources of discomfort. A situation like this makes learning difficult. The teacher may get through the lesson, but he is not getting through to his students. Unsuitable furniture is also a source of discomfort. Many times a classroom will only have folding chairs for the students and a worn out podium for the teacher! The arrangement suggests lecture and a boring lecture with little discussion is usually the result. There are times when desks for the teacher and the students cannot be purchased. But too often the case is otherwise. No one can see the need for desks or tables. "A matter of luxury," they say. "We must be careful with the Lord's money." But if teaching our children the Scriptures is not a part of the Lord's work—then what is? Are we saving pennies only to lose souls later? Every educator knows that discomfort is the cousin of disinterest. It could be that discomfort is the reason your students are not as attentive as they should be. Next time we will have more tips on disinterest and how to overcome it.

Some Suggestions

If you have been reviewing the apostles' chart every week (lesson one), now is when your efforts are rewarded. Your students should have little trouble matching the name of an apostle with the man himself. The name should mean something to them after you finish this week's lesson.

Notes

Teaching Lesson 4

All of the twelve apostles are talked about in this lesson. Some of the more familiar apostles are discussed in detail in the lessons to come. Because of this, it would be good to emphasize the minor or obscure apostles. These are the ones of which we know the least.

Some of the apostles had the same name. This might be a problem area. To overcome it, write the name on the blackboard and list one point or two under each name. For example when studying James, you could do this:

James	
James The Fisherman	**James the Less**
John, his brother	**May have been a short man**
Zebedee, his father	**Alphaeus, his father**
First apostle to die	

The same approach could be taken for Judas and for the two Simons. Contrast helps us to see more clearly.

Lesson 5

The Training of the Twelve

Notes

The Aim

- To know how the twelve were prepared for their important work as apostles.
- To feel that as disciples we, too, should be like our Master who is Jesus.
- To do. Be able to tell why a person cannot really witness for Jesus today.

The second law of teaching is: The student must attend with interest to the material being taught. Teaching accomplishes nothing when interest is lacking. It is the teacher who has the responsibility to arouse and hold the interest of his pupils. Thorough preparation on the part of the teacher is the best remedy for disinterest. The teacher who knows his material well usually has a good class. But sometimes disinterest is because of other reasons which are likewise under the control of the teacher.

There are times when disinterest is because of a disorderly classroom. The room is crowded with materials and furniture that is seldom used. The walls are cluttered with charts and maps. The interest of the student is hampered or distracted in such a situation. Often the room is simply not big enough. What can be done about the seating arrangement if the room is small? Below are two sketches which illustrate how to make the best use of available space in a classroom.

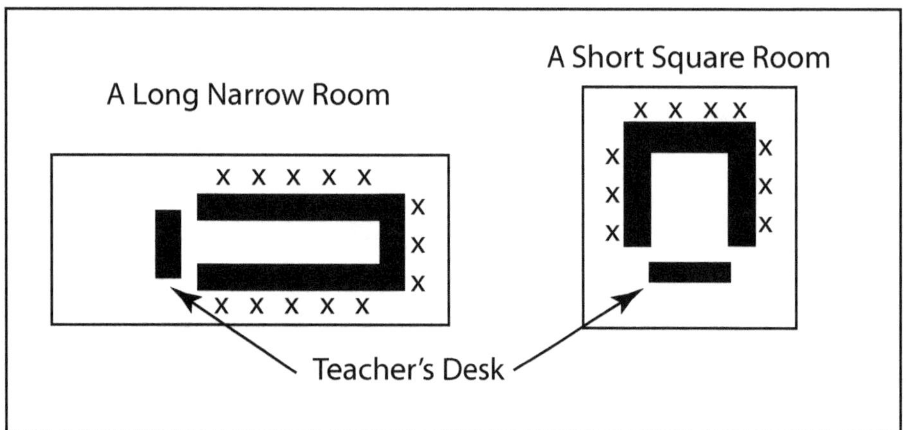

The teacher now has enough room in which to move freely. No student is on any back row. And the teacher can see every student at once. The students themselves are not crowded and a writing surface is right there for them to use. The complete arrangement suggests discussion rather than lecture.

Sometimes interest is lost because the teaching becomes too repeti-

Notes

tious—it becomes stagnant. The students are soon bored; their interest is lost. A teacher can always capture his students' attention and hold it by being enthusiastic. He can use lively facial expressions and appropriate gestures. When you sense you're beginning to lose the interest of your students, that's the time for change! Get up and walk around. Use the blackboard. Ask a question that makes a student commit himself: "Do you think the apostles were common men or extraordinary men when Jesus chose them? Why?"

Some Suggestions

There are times when it is good to take a poll. Ask a question of your class before the lesson is taught. Put the results of the poll on the black-board. On this lesson you might ask: (1) Were the apostles common men? and (2) Can we witness for Christ today? Your blackboard diagram might look like this:

	Yes	No
Apostles: Common men	5	2
Witness for Christ	6	2

Teaching Lesson 5

The memory verse (Acts 4:13) might be a little bewildering. The word "ignorant" has changed in meaning since the KJV was produced. A better rendering would be: "They were uneducated, common men" (RSV).

On the age of the apostles, you might ask: "How many of you have parents who are about thirty years old?" There will probably be several who do. Show that the apostles were about the same age as their parents are.

The Limited Commission, the seventy who were sent out, and the Great Commission are frequently confused. The Limited Commission was limited to the Jews alone (Matt. 10:5,6). The seventy were sent before the Lord as He went to Jerusalem for the last time (Luke 9:51; 10:1). The Great Commission was given by the risen Christ for all the world (Matt. 28:18-20).

Lesson 6

Simon Peter

Notes

The Aim

- To know the life of the apostle called Peter.
- To feel the weaknesses and the strength of Peter and how he was human just as we are.
- To do. When we fail spiritually, to learn to be like Peter and return to God.

Discipline in a classroom can be a problem. What should be done with the noisy unruly child? Should a teacher harshly scold his class? Probably no one really has the right answer. Each new group of students you will teach will be different; each class seems to assume a personality all of its own. But one thing is certain. There must be discipline in a class, if any teaching is to be done. But there is another side to the coin, too. A class that is constantly threatened with discipline is not good either. It's like the sword of Damocles hanging over your head. The teacher who must repeatedly threaten to send his students to their parents will not be an effective teacher. The atmosphere is not conducive to learning. What can be done?

Try never to let a class become so uncontrolled that a good scolding is necessary. Deal with small problems while they are small. For example, if you have two students who like to visit with one another during class, simply say, "I don't want you to be talking like that in class." And then go on. There's no need to make a big issue; you've probably solved the problem right then.

Just as thorough preparation on the part of the teacher is the best remedy for disinterest, it is also the best way to avoid discipline problems. Many times it is the teacher who is at fault and not the students. A little humor should help, too. Children have a natural sense of humor. Humor relaxes the mind and gives you, the teacher, an opportunity to drive a point home. Humor eases any tension that might be in the air and makes learning much easier.

Teaching Lesson 6

The main point of lesson six is Peter's confession (Matt. 16:16). It is important that the student understands what the word "Christ" means. He may be surprised to learn that Christ was not Jesus' last name. "Christ" means "anointed." There were three offices in the Old Testament which were identified by anointing: priest, prophet, king. Jesus is all three (priest, prophet, king) in one. Also, the "rock" which Jesus talked about deserves attention. The "rock" cannot be Peter (1 Cor. 3:1 1). The "rock" is the confession that Peter made. If Jesus were not the Christ, no church could have been built.

The warmth of Peter's personality is one of the most touching stories of the New Testament. Everyone can see a little of himself in Peter. Perhaps, this is why Peter seems so human and so alive. Here is a

Notes

golden opportunity for character development. You will want to stress both the weaknesses and the strength of Peter's character. Ask the class what they would have done had they been Peter and had seen Jesus transfigured. Or, "Why do you think Peter denied that he knew Jesus?"

The lesson of the transfiguration is that we are to hear Jesus today. You may want to read Deuteronomy 5:2, 3 in class. Horeb is another name for Sinai.

The Aim

Lesson 7

James

Notes

- To know the life of the apostle called James.
- To feel that serving or helping one another is a noble thing because this is what Jesus wants.
- To do. To learn to be faithful unto death as James was.

The third law of teaching is: The language used in teaching must be common to both the teacher and the pupil. This means that teaching is a two way street. The teacher and his students must share a common road of vocabulary. The words they use must carry the same meaning for both of them.

A word can have several meanings. Take the word "court," for example. It sounds simple enough and is not hard to spell. But "court" can mean many different things. A teacher may be talking about a *court* of the Jews. A student immediately thinks of a *court*yard rather than an assembly which administers justice. Another student may think of a *court*room; and another, of a tennis *court*. You may even have one student who is a little romantic. She thinks of love and an act of wooing. Words need to be defined in context.

Problems of language can also result because the teacher uses long, involved sentences. He talks on and on. Or, the teacher mutters and cannot be easily heard or understood. This too is a language problem.

The solution is an easy one. Use simple words. Use short sentences. And closely observe your students. When you see they do not understand, back up and try a different route. Use a different word or a different illustration. Or try to diagram what you're talking about on the black-board.

The teacher who constantly lectures to his students will not be aware of any language problems. This is the serious drawback to lecturing. It is only through discussion that language problems are clearly seen. Discussion corrects misunderstanding. Discussion focuses the camera of teaching.

Some Suggestions

A panel discussion is an easy way to overcome language problems. Students have little trouble communicating with one another. A panel discussion takes advantage of this. It also stirs and creates interests in a classroom. Below (Teaching Lesson Seven) is an example on how to conduct a panel discussion. Here are some other suggestions. If possible, bring a small table into your classroom. Have two or three students volunteer to be on the panel. The other students will ask questions and the panel will be responsible for answering. The students who are not on the panel should be given about five minutes to write several questions in advance. Now you are ready to begin.

Notes

Teaching Lesson 7

The class is forty-five minutes. Our plan is to spend the first fifteen minutes in light discussion. This will be done by the teacher and the students. The last thirty minutes will be student panel discussion.

Teacher: "Everyone close your books and your Bibles. We want you to meet our panel of apostle experts. They are . . . (give their names). The panel will reply to your questions about this lesson or any other lesson we have covered on the apostles. You must tell whether the reply of the panel is true or false. This is like our true-false questions that are in the book. Johnny Student, you may ask the first question. Then it will be Mary's turn. When everyone has asked a question, we'll start again with Johnny."

Johnny: "Who was the father of James?" Panel: "Zebedee." Johnny: "That's right." Mary: "Why does our lesson describe James as a fiery comet?" Panel: "Because he had bright red hair." (Laughter). Mary: "That's false." Teacher: "Does anyone know how James was like a comet?" The discussion continues.

The teacher supplements the questions asked by his students and stresses the important points of the lesson.

Lesson 8

John

Notes

The Aim

- To know the life of the apostle called John.
- To feel the necessity to honor our parents.
- To do. To learn to be concerned about those we teach as Jesus was.

The fourth law of teaching is: The truth to be taught must be learned through truth already known. Teaching is going from the known to the unknown. Or to put it another way, teaching is building bridges—not just telling facts. A good teacher discovers what his students already know and teaches from there. He builds bridges.

The Lord Himself used this principle. His parables are excellent examples of teaching the unknown by the known. The word "parable" literally means "that which is thrown along side of something else." A "parable" is a spiritual fact (the unknown) that is thrown along side of a physical fact (the known). It is teaching the unknown by the known. This is why the parables of Jesus were so effective.

A good teacher knows his students well. He knows their names and something about them. He can tell you what they know about the Bible. It is this personal knowledge which gives him a bridge head from which to teach.

Once the teacher knows his students, then he is in a position to determine the possible unknown factors in a lesson. This can be done in just a few minutes. Read the lesson. Ask yourself, "What points may be unfamiliar to my students? Are there some ideas that are new or that may not be clear to them?" List the points and be prepared to answer them or explain them more completely.

Some Suggestions

Crossword puzzles can be a spark to kindle the fire of interest. They are easy to write and can be drawn on a blackboard in minutes. Squares can be made the same size by tracing the shape of a book with chalk. Draw one square; move the book and draw another square.

Notes

There is a crossword puzzle at the end of lesson eight. It could be used as a starter. By putting it on the blackboard, you have plenty of room to add more questions and squares. Make the puzzle a class project.

Teaching Lesson 8

John and Peter were good friends. Both had once been fishermen. They must have worked hard for a living. Their faces were probably weather-beaten and their hands calloused. Here is where a picture of fishermen fishing with nets would be good. Many students may think of fishing only as a sport rather than an occupation!

One of the vital points of this lesson is children honoring their parents. "Honor" means more than mere respect. 1 Timothy 5:3 will help to explain the meaning of honor: "Honor widows who are really widows." Verses 8 and 16 show that "honoring" means to provide for them and to help them.

The last paragraph of lesson eight (The Disciple Whom Jesus Loved) demands a little reviewing on the part of the teacher. You will need to be able to tell the following stories quickly and clearly: (1) Jesus and Nicodemus (John 3); (2) Jesus and the Samaritan woman (John 4); (3) Jesus and the lame man in Jerusalem (John 5). All three are examples of how Jesus taught others. It is important that the student understands that Jesus was personally concerned about those whom He taught.

Lesson 9
Andrew

Notes

The Aim

- To know the life of the apostle called Andrew.
- To feel the importance of bringing someone to Jesus.
- To do. To be like Andrew by bringing someone to class with us.

The fifth law of teaching is: The teacher must direct the self-activites of his pupils. Teaching is not just telling facts or covering the questions at the end of each lesson. An important part of teaching is getting the pupil to respond and to do so freely. It is this response on the part of the student that transforms the abstract into the concrete—the unpractical into the practical. Response is what gives teaching meaning. It burns the lesson into the mind of the student. The teacher's responsibility can be summed up in three points.

A teacher must stimulate thinking. He must not only provide material for thought (fact-telling), but also direct the student to do his own thinking. This is aiming for response. Never tell your students what they can learn for themselves. Instead, lead them to a conclusion. Offer suggestions that are nothing more than signs along the highway to learning. Stimulate their thinking. How?

A teacher must arouse a spirit of inquiry. Keep asking your students for the "why" of things. Questions are the secret to effective teaching. What? How? Why? When? Where? Who? These are the things a teacher must constantly ask. Many people think of teaching as a teacher telling facts with eager students asking questions. But it is really the other way around. It is the teacher who must ask questions which make his students tell the facts. The point to remember is that you are not teaching the Bible, you are teaching students.

A teacher must get his pupils to work. For younger children, this means at the end of a lesson have them color pictures or do some other type of hand work. When coloring is used in this manner, it is neither a time killer nor entertainment. It becomes a part of teaching. The teacher must provide an opportunity for his pupils to put into practice what they have learned. For older students this means: research projects, panel discussions, completing written questions, and even student-teaching. The learning process must be an active one; it cannot be passive. There is something that the student himself must do, if he is to learn. And this is the teacher's challenge and his responsibility.

Some Suggestions

If you made the suggested chart on the apostles (lesson one). you will want to keep referring to it. Repetition is the best teacher. One thing you might do with the chart is remove it or turn it around so that it cannot be seen. Then, have your students repeat the chart from memory. This could be done as a class project. The class could say the names of the apostles from memory while one student wrote the names on the

Notes

blackboard. This is an excellent way of getting your students to work.

Teaching Lesson 9

The following is an example of how a teacher might ask and use questions in teaching a class. Notice that the questions, for the most part, are directed to the class as a whole. No one student is singled out from the rest. It is class discussion with class participation that is wanted. The class is forty-five minutes. Our plan is to spend thirty minutes in an exhaustive discussion. The last fifteen minutes will be used to answer the questions in our lesson book.

(The chart on the apostles has been reviewed by the class.) Teacher: "This week our lesson is on Andrew, isn't it? Who was Andrew's brother?" Student: "Peter." Teacher: "Was Peter better known than Andrew?" No reply. Teacher (writes on the blackboard: Matt. 10:2; Luke 6:14; John 6:8): "Let's look at these passages in our Bibles. See if you can see how they are alike." (Pause). Student: "All three say that Andrew was Peter's brother." Teacher: "Peter is never described as Andrew's brother. Is he?" The discussion continues.

Notes

Lesson 10

Thomas

The Aim

- To know the life of the apostle called Thomas.
- To feel the tragic loss of the apostles when Jesus died.
- To do. Be able to tell why Thomas was not some professional doubter or skeptic.

The sixth law of teaching is: The pupil must reproduce in his own mind the truths to be learned. The learning process is a progressive one. It begins with rote memorization and ends with response. Response is where the lesson taught is reproduced in the life of the student. Between rote and response are two other steps: understanding and relation. The entire process would resemble a stair way.

There are some educators who view learning as a five step process. This is accomplished by subdividing one of the four steps diagramed above. An explanation of each of the steps is as follows:

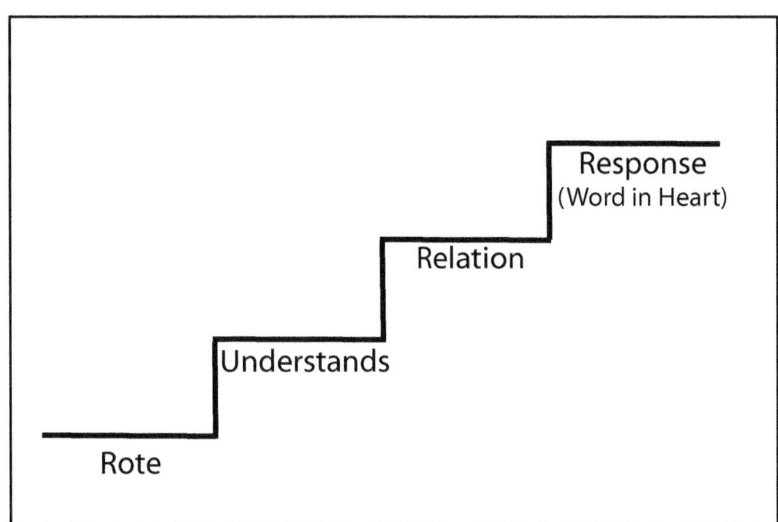

1. Rote or memorization is the first step. It is also the lowest level of learning. The student merely repeats facts from memory. An example would be saying the names of the apostles or the books of the Bible. Rote is an important level of learning, but is incomplete by itself. Unfortunately, all that some teachers require is rote memorization on the part of the student.

2. Understanding is the second level of learning. Here the student retells or restates the lesson in his own words. He has mastered the content of the lesson and can reproduce it. Multiple choice questions, fill in the blanks, and true-false are all examples of the second level of learning. The student recognizes what he has been taught.

3. Relation is the level of learning where application of what has been taught comes into focus. Here the student is able to see the

Notes

relation of what he has learned to other facts—including his own life. The lesson suddenly becomes practical. The relation step is as far as the teacher can go. The next level is up to the student.

4. Response is the highest level of learning. On the response level the student applies what he has learned to his own life. The character sketches of the apostles (which the teacher has been teaching all along) now becomes part of the character of the student. The lesson taught is seen in the life of the student. This is the end of teaching and this is its goal.

Teaching Lesson 10

Thomas is remembered as the apostle who doubted. But what is forgotten is that all of the apostles doubted the resurrection of Jesus. It is quite common for the world to teach that a man who doubts is superior to others. The doubter is looked upon as more intelligent or more honest than other men. But there is no virtue in doubting or being an atheist. Be certain to stress this point. It is imperative that the student understands why Thomas and the others doubted. The last paragraph of lesson ten discusses this in detail. Here's an excellent opportunity to show the relationship between faith and the New Testament.

It would also be good to trace the life of Thomas by following the subheadings of the lesson. These are easily recognized as they are set in bold type. Go through the life of Thomas by using the subheadings as an outline. The memory verse is also rich but needs to be worked and mined.

Lesson 11

Matthew

The Aim

- To know the life of the apostle called Matthew.
- To feel that the gospel is for all people.
- To do. To be willing to leave everything behind to follow Jesus, as Matthew did.

The seventh law of teaching is: The completion of the work of teaching must be made by review and application. Review is an important part of teaching. Repetition is the best teacher and review is repetition. The real test of teaching is not how much we give our students, but how much they retain. The student will naturally retain or remember more if the teacher reviews regularly.

Review is not the last five minutes of class when everything else has been studied. This does not mean that a summary by the teacher near the end of a class is not good. It is. But a summary should be planned and utilized as a part of teaching. Summaries should not be looked upon as time fillers. Review can also be done at the beginning of a lesson. Important points from previous lessons can be covered again. Also, parts of the lesson being taught can be reviewed during the class period. Review is something that can be done at the beginning, the middle, and the end of a lesson. A good pattern to follow in teaching is: review, teach, review the point taught, and summarize all the points covered at the end of the lesson.

The value of review is that it enables a teacher to know what his pupils have learned. What does this mean? The teacher certainly knows what he has taught in class—but what his pupils actually learned is quite another point. Review tells the teacher what facts of the lesson his pupils failed to grasp. It gives the teacher the opportunity to fill in any gaps and to correct wrong impressions that may have occurred in the lesson. The best reason for review lies in the power of repetition. Repetition is the best teacher.

Some Suggestions

The lesson on Matthew is a little shorter than many of the previous lessons. This should give you, the teacher, an excellent chance to review. The crossword puzzle at the end of the lesson is a puzzle on review. Almost all of the questions are about apostles you have already studied. You might want to write some additional review questions to ask your students.

Teaching Lesson 11

The meaning of the word "publican" may be a little obscure. In the lesson, "publican" and "tax-gatherer" are used as synonyms. This should give the general thought. A *publican* was a *tax-gatherer.* He was hated by the people of his day because many publicans were dishonest. Sometimes publicans collected taxes on a percentage basis the

Notes

Notes

more taxes they collected, the more money they made. You will want to show that Matthew was a publican, but he was never described as dishonest.

Some students may have trouble understanding how Matthew and Levi could be the same man. A good way to explain this might be with a question. "How many of you have a second or middle name?" Or, you might refer to someone who is known by a nickname.

The banquet Matthew held in Jesus' honor is an important lesson. Have your students read the account from the Bible (Matt. 9:9-13). The last paragraph of the lesson discusses the banquet in detail. Ask your class, "Do you think Jesus was saying that bad people should be our best friends?" Another good question is: "Did the Pharisees need a doctor as well as the publicans and sinners?" The point Jesus was making is that He had come to save all men. This is the lesson of the Great Commission which Jesus will give later (Mark 16:15).

Lesson 12
Judas

Notes

The Aim

- To know the life of the apostle called Judas.
- To feel that the love of money is the root of all evil.
- To do. To love other Christians and be willing to do things for them. To know that this is why Jesus washed the feet of His apostles.

Teaching is more than lecture or fact-telling. Teaching means more than imparting information. The student is the very heart of teaching. He is why the lesson is taught. It is the student which makes teaching important. And it is the student which gives teaching life. The good teacher seeks to change the life of his student by what he teaches. His goal is to mold the lives of his pupils—to give them vision and a sense of direction. His aim is to develop character.

KNOWLEDGE
WHAT THE PUPIL KNOWS

ATTITUDE
HOW THE PUPIL FEELS

ACTION
WHAT THE PUPIL DOES

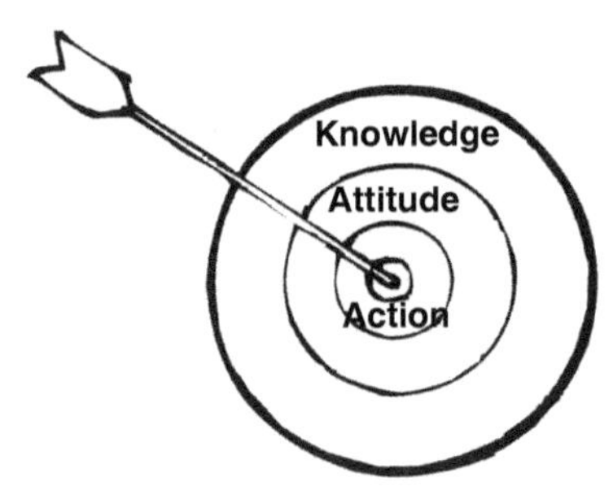

Teaching is effective only when it changes lives. The Lord's illustration of the wise man and the foolish man reflects this very point (Matt. 7:24-27). The foolish man built his house on the sand, but the wise man built his house upon a rock. Jesus explained that the foolish man only heard His sayings, while the wise man both heard and did. The difference was in doing. Learning, like teaching, is effective only when it changes life.

Teaching which changes life has three aims: knowledge, attitude, and action. What do I want the pupil to know (the facts of a lesson)? What do I want the pupil to feel (the attitudes)? And what do I want the

Notes

pupil to do (the actions in life)? Teaching is more than knowledge—teaching is changing the life of a child.

Teaching Lesson 12

The life of Judas is difficult to explain and to teach. It is hard to understand how a man who knew Jesus well could have betrayed the Master. Judas had been with Jesus for nearly three years. He had walked with Jesus, heard Him teach, and seen Him perform miracles. He and the Lord even ate out of the same dish. Judas did not become an apostle so he could betray Jesus in the end. When Judas first followed Jesus, he wanted to do right and live a good life. He wanted to be righteous. But somehow, somewhere along the way, Judas changed.

Ask your class, "How many of you would name a baby 'Judas'?" Show that there was a time when Judas had been a noble name. Jesus even had a brother named Jude or Judas. But after Judas betrayed Jesus, the name of Judas came to mean shame and disgrace. This is how bad the treachery of Judas was.

Does your class know why Judas was called "Iscariot"? A man from Texas is sometimes called a Texan. Judas was called "Iscariot" because he was from Kerioth, Judaea.

Why did Judas betray Jesus? Was it because he loved money? That's certainly part of the answer. But Judas also scorned Jesus. The price he asked was an insult. Be certain to stress how much thirty pieces of silver are worth. Imagine, Judas sold Jesus for thirty pieces of silver. Do some research to see what that would buy in today's economy.

Matthias took the place of Judas. Matthias was studied in lesson one but a review is certainly in order here.

Lesson 13
Paul

Notes

The Aim

- To know the life of the apostle called Paul.
- To feel the zeal of Paul as he labored and suffered for the Lord.
- To do. To be as devout as Paul was.

The type of teaching that changes life is not an accident. It doesn't just happen. The teacher who is effective is the teacher who has worked on his teaching. He has developed his ability to teach in addition to knowing his material well. This is the difference between the good teacher and the poor or ineffective teacher. The poor teacher either does not know his material well enough or he does not know how to present his material. Some people who teach will always be better teachers than others. This is true in anything we do. But it is also true that, with conscious effort, every teacher can become a better teacher. The following are some works that may help you to improve your teaching. Some of the material suggested contains religious error and must therefore be recommended with caution.

Lawrence Richards, *Creative Bible Teaching.* An excellent work on the principles of teaching.

Teaching with All Your Heart, David E. Fessenden

Effective Bible Teaching, Jim Wilhoit & Leland Ryken

A Generation That Knows Not God, Bob and Sandra Waldron

Relevance? Or Humanism?, Bob and Sandra Waldron

Teaching Lesson 13

No study of the apostles would be complete unless Paul was also included. But the study of Paul also creates a problem. No single lesson can do justice to the life of Paul. There is simply too much material—too many points to cover. This means that, in teaching the life of Paul, you must be selective. Everything cannot be taught. The most important points must be sought out and stressed. Here are some suggestions on how to teach the life of Paul.

List the missionary or preaching journeys on the blackboard. Tell where each journey began and where it ended. Also mention why the journey was taken. Help the student to identify each journey by discussing something important that happened on the journey. Then go to the next point.

The conversion of Paul needs to be emphasized. Paul was not saved on the road to Damascus. Ananias told Saul to be baptized and wash away his sins (Acts 22:16). This was three days after Paul had seen the risen Christ.

Another point is the apostleship of Paul. He was an apostle to the Gentiles. (Review lesson one.) His authority as an apostle was equal to the authority of the twelve apostles.

www.ingramcontent.com/pod-product-compliance
Lightning Source LLC
LaVergne TN
LVHW081317060426
835509LV00015B/1565
9781584272885